IVIES

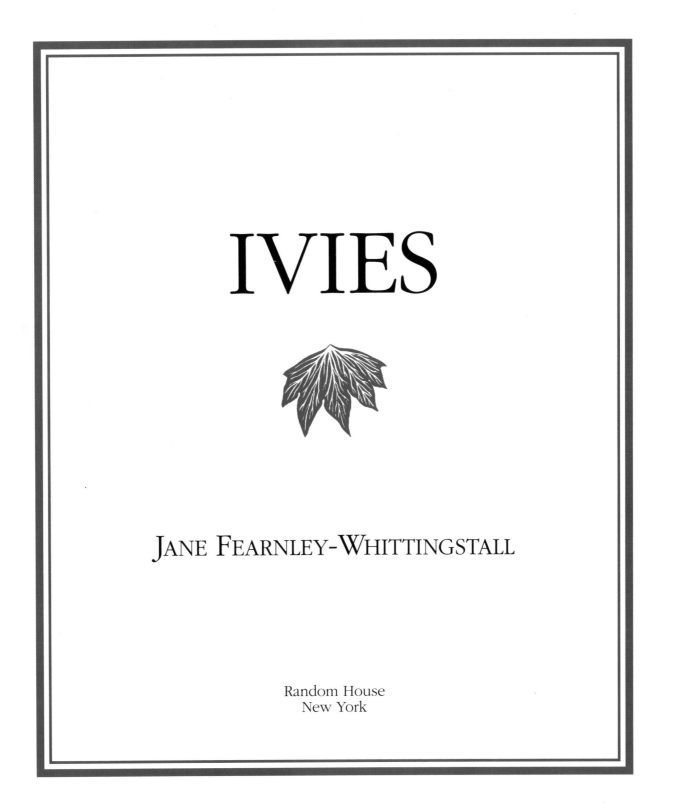

Jane Fearnley-Whittingstall

Random House
New York

This work was originally published in
Great Britain by Chatto & Windus, Ltd., London.

Library of Congress Cataloging-in-Publication Data

Fearnley-Whittingstall, Jane.
    Ivies / by Jane Fearnley-Whittingstall
      p. cm.
    Includes index.
    ISBN 0-679-41231-X
    1. Ivy.   I. Title.
SB413.I84F43 1991
635.9'74 -- dc20   91-51024

Manufactured in Great Britain

24689753

First U.S. edition

Editor Lizzie Boyd
Design Margaret Sadler
Picture research Philippa Lewis

OPPOSITE TITLE PAGE *Ivy leaf magnified to show lateral veins.*
DEDICATION PAGE Hedera helix *'Buttercup' partially clothing
a stone sphinx in a private garden in Dublin.*
OPPOSITE CONTENTS PAGE *Ivies contribute to a harmony of foliage
textures at Isola Bella in Italy.*

For JHL

What's your name?
Something that clings
What, mud?
No, ivy.

CONTENTS

INTRODUCTION

*Even the most ordinary plants will take on
a new significance if you will refuse the
associations that spring to mind and try to
see their form, texture and colour as though
for the first time.*
Russell Page, *The Education of a Gardener*

PREVIOUS PAGE
*The evening light
catches* Hedera
colchica *'Sulphur
Heart' at Barnsley
House, Gloucester-
shire.*

ABOVE *A detail
from* Still Life with
Flowers *by John
Wainwright
(1859).*

RIGHT *Winter
colour on the
leaves of* Hedera
helix.

Ivy is a plant of almost miraculous versatility and
adaptability. The larger ivies will cover a wall
with shapely evergreen leaves to a height of 100ft
(30m) or more, without support; the smallest will
clothe the pebbles of a doll's house-sized grotto
in a bottle or terrarium. Some ivy leaves are the
size of dinner plates, others are no bigger than
the nail of a little finger.

Yet ivy does not have a glamorous image.
Many gardeners consider it at worst a destructive
nuisance and at best as a last-ditch remedy for
places where nothing else will grow. It also has
an undeserved reputation as a funereal plant. Yet
its leaves have a gloss that reflects light on even
the dullest of days, and the variegated forms
bring an impression of sunlight to the darkest
corners of our gardens. Ivies come not only in

every shade of green but also touched with grey,
yellow, cream, pink and purple, in every con-
ceivable variegation and pattern – streaked,
splashed, spotted, speckled, edged, mottled,
marbled, veined. In texture and shape the leaves
can be crimped and ruffled, smooth and rounded
or sharply pointed and deeply divided.

Ivies will climb, trail, form dense ground cover
or make sturdy shrubs. They are stoic survivors,
many varieties tolerating extremes of heat and
cold, dense shade and atmospheric pollution.
They will grow in most soils and will survive
droughts, snow and frost. They thrive indoors
and outside. There are ivies to suit the bathroom
shelf and ivies to adorn the landscaped park.

The grace of ivy tendrils and the delicate veining of the leaves show an elegance that belies its
robust constitution. What other plant can put on
such a brave show of beauty all the year round
both in the mass seen from a distance, and close
up in the individual leaf or spray? And often in
adverse conditions.

Why do so few gardeners exploit such qualities? Is it the plant's unperturbable tenacity, and
the very fact that it will grow in unfriendly sites
where nothing else can survive that makes us
take it for granted? Instead of enjoying ivies we
tuck them away in dark corners and forget them.
But they never sulk. They quietly get on with the
task of covering the potting shed, hiding a tree
stump, or colonizing a stony bank.

Indoors, too, ivies provide invaluable, living decoration for homes and places of work. They also play an important role as protectors against indoor air pollution: according to research carried out by NASA *Hedera helix* destroys benzene, a carcinogen present in paints, solvents and cigarette smoke.

Fortunately there are signs that the period of neglect for the Cinderella of the garden is at an end. A reassessment of ivies has been taking place. Apostles of ivy have banded together to form the American Ivy Society and the British Ivy Society, and their work in spreading the ivy gospel has resulted in rapidly growing membership of both organizations. The work of the societies has been invaluable in sorting out the confusion that has existed over the naming of ivy varieties for the past hundred years. It is now possible to compile accurate lists and descriptions of those ivies that are officially recognized, and to relate them to the unofficial synonyms under which many of them are still marketed.

Ivies are already widely appreciated in North America and Japan for use in houses, gardens and large-scale landscape projects. In Mediterranean countries where the cool, green shade of foliage plants has always been valued, ivies can be seen everywhere. However, even in these countries only a small number of the immense range of available ivies is in common use.

It is hoped that this book may inspire new enthusiasts to join the brotherhood of ivy addicts and encourage those who are already converted to experiment more widely with the rich variety of effects that ivy can provide. The easiest of plants to cultivate, ivies are also among the most rewarding.

Ivy as ground cover in a formal avenue.

1

Ivy
and its
Mythology

Ivy's preferred habitat is shady or semi-shaded woodland, where its natural form of growth is to creep along the ground, sending out shoots that root as they go. When the shoots encounter a vertical obstacle, such as a tree trunk or wall, they begin to climb by means of hairy, adhesive rootlets and ivy has been known to reach a height of 100 feet (30m) or more. Where the ground or a retaining wall falls away, ivy will trail gracefully downwards without producing rootlets on its stems.

While ivies have the great advantage, from the gardener's point of view, that they will tolerate shade, most will also grow in full sun, although their growth will then be slower and more wiry and compact. They stand up well to drought and are tolerant of pollution.

The greenish-yellow flowers are held in hemispherical clusters and appear in the autumn. They develop into small, round, green fruits which turn blue-black with a grape-like bloom as they ripen. In a few, rare varieties, including the poet's ivy (*Hedera helix* 'Poetica'), the berries are golden-yellow or orange.

When ivy is about to flower for the first time, the plant undergoes an extraordinary metamorphosis. Towards the top of the plant new, adult leaves develop which are quite different in shape from the juvenile leaves, the margins being smooth and without the pointed lobes which are typical of the juvenile leaves on most ivies. Eventually the new leaf form takes over the whole plant, and the habit of growth also alters. The plant ceases climbing and begins to behave like a shrub, putting out stout branches instead of climbing or trailing tendrils. Having once undergone these changes, the plant will flower every year and continue to grow and develop in its adult, shrubby or arborescent form.

In effect, each ivy has the potential to be two completely different plants: a self-clinging climber and a bushy shrub. The latter, arborescent form, often known as tree ivy, retains its shrubby character when propagated from cuttings. This is the only method of obtaining tree ivies for garden shrubs and hedging plants, as seeds from the ivies

PREVIOUS PAGE
Classical Herm against an ivy wall.

ABOVE Hedera helix *'Buttercup' in the branches of an arbutus.*

Hedera is the Latin name for the genus of plants which is commonly known as ivy to the English-speaking world, *lierre* to the French and *Efeu* to the Germans. A hardy, evergreen climbing shrub, it is a familiar sight in many parts of the world, being native to a region stretching from Japan in the East to the Azores in the West, and from southern Scandinavia in the North to as far south as North Africa. It also thrives as an introduced plant in the Americas and in Australasia.

will produce climbing plants. It is not fully understood what stimulus causes an ivy to burgeon into maturity. It seems to occur most frequently when the climber has reached the top of its support although it also sometimes occurs on ivies creeping on the ground.

Hedera helix, the ivy native to Europe (usually sold by nurseries under the name 'English ivy') has another intriguing quality. It has an astonishing ability to 'sport' or throw out mutant shoots that are quite different from the parent plant. They are often highly ornamental rather than freakish, and this is how many attractive varieties, with unusually shaped or colourfully variegated leaves, first occurred.

Ivy can live to a great age. The idea of its longevity has often attracted poets, among them Lord Byron who wrote in *Childe Harold:*

There is a stern round tower of other days,
Firm as a fortress, with its fence of stone,
Such as an army's baffled strength delays,
Standing with half its battlements alone,
And with two thousand years of ivy grown,
The garland of eternity, where wave
The green leaves over all by time o'erthrown.

An ivy 2000 years old would be very remarkable, and allowance should be made for poetic licence in Byron's case, but an ivy at least 400 years old has been recorded growing at Ginac, near Montpellier in France, and the ivies planted by the 1866 graduating class on the walls of Princeton University are still going strong.

FALSE ACCUSATIONS

Over the centuries ivy has acquired an undeserved bad name. Even when it was at the height of its popularity as an ornamental plant, towards the end of the nineteenth century, a Professor Freeman referred to it as 'That baleful plant, that insidious weed.' He was deceived by two accusations against ivy which can be firmly denied. One is that it is poisonous. It is not poisonous to ani-

mals in any of its parts. Cattle and horses will browse on ivy when there is nothing more succulent available and it does them no harm. Indeed, archaeologists have found evidence that ivy was gathered by men as winter fodder for the earliest domesticated animals 5000 years ago. Going back even further, prehistoric man probably fed wild game animals on ivy in the same way.

The only part of the plant which is mildly poisonous to humans is the seed, which has been used medicinally as a purgative. The idea that ivy leaves are poisonous may have gained credence because the plant has been confused with another climber commonly known as 'Poison Ivy': *Rhus radicans,* sometimes wrongly listed as *Rhus toxicodendron,* is a deciduous climber with vivid red autumn colour, native to North America and Mexico. The poison is in the sap which can cause very serious blistering to the skin. The plant's resemblance to *Hedera* is merely superficial and

ABOVE LEFT *The flowers and seed-heads of* Hedera helix *in its adult arborescent form.*

ABOVE RIGHT *A spray of adult ivy-bearing fruit, from* The Grammar of Ornament *by Owen Jones (1868).*

7

then the ivy shoots will intrude and aggravate the faults as they grow. For the same reason, ivy should never be allowed to grow into the guttering or roof tiles of a building and should be kept away from window frames where shoots might prise their way between the frame and the wall.

If you are in any doubt as to whether a brick wall is sound enough to support ivy, you can test the strength of the mortar by scraping it with a key or knife. If the mortar crumbles, before you introduce ivy to the wall you should have it repointed with a mortar mix of cement : hydrated lime : sand in the ratio 1:1:6. Alternatively, the ivy can be trained to a trellis set a few inches out from the wall.

When ivy has taken hold of an old, damaged wall, it is sometimes unwise to pull it off, as the ivy may be the one thing that is holding the wall up. Ivy on the sound walls of a building is not only harmless, but has a positive advantage. It provides excellent insulation, its cover being dense enough to limit heat loss through the walls. The leaves are so angled downwards and outwards as to throw off driving rain and snow, helping to protect the building from damp penetration.

Although the top growth is harmless, there is a slight risk to house foundations from the underground roots of ivy, though no more than with other climbing plants. There is a story that the questing roots of an ancient ivy growing on the walls of Magdalen College at Oxford University found their way through weak masonry into the cellar. Their thirst led the roots to a bottle of vintage port, and they pushed the cork in and drank the contents, leaving the bottle filled with a mass of roots. History does not relate whether the drunken ivy wilted or grew with renewed vigour, nor how the dons of the College reacted to their sad loss.

As far as trees are concerned, ivy is not a parasite and will not hurt a host tree unless it is very old, weak or diseased. In that case ivy that has reached its adult phase at the top of a tree can rob it of light so that it cannot survive, or it can make the tree so top-heavy that it comes down in a strong gale. It is a wise precaution, when trees are

ABOVE *'Boston Ivy' (Virginia Creeper) showing autumn colour in the Cotswolds.*

OPPOSITE *The weight of the ivy puts this tree at risk from strong winds.*

unlikely to confuse anyone who encounters it. The leaves consist of three leaflets, flowers are borne in summer and the berries are white.

The second accusation against ivy has given it an enduring but false reputation for damaging walls and killing trees. Ivy cannot harm a sound wall since the rootlets which attach it to the wall are not true roots and do not penetrate in search of moisture or nutrients. However, if the mortar in the joints is loose or there are cracks in the wall,

exposed to strong winds, to trim any ivy growing on their trunks every few years so that it does not reach the crown of the tree and does not develop its adult form.

An interesting experiment carried out in oak woodland owned by Winchester College has shown that healthy trees are not affected by ivy. Starting in 1890, half the trees were cleaned of ivy at ten-year intervals, and the other half were left with ivy on them. When they were felled in 1942 no difference was found in height, girth or average cubic content.

IMPOSTORS

ABOVE *The gnarled and knotted branches of an ancient ivy.*

RIGHT *The larva of a Holly-Blue butterfly feeding on an ivy berry.*

Apart from the 'Poison Ivy' mentioned above there are several other plants commonly called 'Ivy' which are no relation to *Hedera* whatsoever. The best known is 'Boston Ivy' *(Parthenocissus tricuspidata),* a deciduous climber also known as Virginia Creeper. It is an excellent vigorous plant,

not poisonous, with leaves somewhere between those of an ivy and a vine, and brilliant red autumn colour. It covers many of the buildings of the American East Coast universities, and it is probably Boston Ivy rather than the true ivy that has earned them the epithet 'Ivy League'.

'Swedish Ivy' *(Plectranthus oertendahlii)* is a tender, evergreen plant from South Africa, which first became popular in Sweden. The waxy, bronze-green leaves have conspicuous white veining and its trailing habit makes it an effective plant for pots and hanging baskets.

Most of the false ivies are tender house plants with the same trailing habit as the true ivy, and are valued for their foliage. The 'Grape Ivy', 'Kangaroo Ivy' and 'Marine Ivy' are all forms of *Cissus*; 'German Ivy', also known as 'Parlour Ivy', is *Senecio mikanioides* and 'Devil's Ivy' is *Scindapsus aureus*.

Ivy has also lent its name to flowering plants with leaves that resemble those of the ivy, such as the ivy-leaved Geranium and ivy-leaved Toadflax. Typical ivy leaves are such a distinctive shape that they are used to describe the leaves of other plants both in English and in botanical Latin, where the epithet *hederifolia* is used.

IVY AND WILD LIFE

Ivy is a good friend to birds, butterflies and insects, especially in its adult form. Flowering as it does late in the year, its blossom provides nectar and pollen for bees and other insects well into November when there is little other food around for them. The Holly-Blue butterfly lays its eggs on the flowers in October, and other butterflies including the Brimstone hibernate in ivy. Peacock and Tortoiseshell butterflies are seen on ivy, and in his book *The Ivy,* first published in 1872, Shirley Hibberd says that Red Admirals, Painted Ladies, Camberwell Beauties and Pearl-Bordered Fritillaries are found on ivy flowers. Alas, most of these are today found only too rarely anywhere.

The ivy berries last until late winter as food for birds:

> *Ivy hath berys as black as any slo*
> *There came the owle and ete him as*
> * she go.*
>
> (old carol)

The branches provide shelter for many birds that feed and nest or roost in the dense foliage including blackbirds, finches, dippers, fieldfares, wag-

tails, hedge sparrows, linnets, thrushes, redwings, robins, treecreepers, willow warblers, woodpigeons, wrens and yellowhammers.

When ivy is stripped from the towers of castles and churches in the name of architectural conservation, an important sanctuary for owls is destroyed:

> *. . . from yonder ivy-mantled tow'r*
> *The moping owl does to the moon complain,*
> *Of such, as wand'ring near her secret bow'r*
> *Molest her ancient solitary reign.*
>
> Thomas Gray, *Elegy Written*
> *in a Country Churchyard*

ABOVE *In winter, ivy provides shelter for birds.*

11

THE GARLAND OF ETERNITY

The distinctive, elegant leaf shape of ivy, its ever-green quality, its ready availability, and the fact that cut branches last well without wilting have led to its ornamental and symbolic use from the earliest times.

In ancient Egypt it was called the plant of Osiris. The god of the Nile, ruler and judge of the under-world, is depicted in sculptures and hieroglyphs carrying an ivy-entwined thyrsus, or staff. The staff and two other traditional attributes of Osiris, the leopard skin and tambourine, were also part of the equipment of Dionysus or Bacchus, the Greek and Roman god of wine.

Dionysus' ivy-covered thyrsus is mentioned by Euripides in *The Bacchae* in lines which in trans-lation read:

On Nyssa's savage-nursing height
Shakest thou thine ivy wand.

The god is often shown wearing a wreath of ivy, and, as part of the ceremonial of his worship, his female devotees, the Maenads or Bacchantes, used to flourish the ivy thyrsus in their proces-sions and orgiastic dances.

In Greek mythology there is a legend that Dionysus, posing as a mortal, was kidnapped by the crew of a ship on which he was travelling to the island of Naxos. He was such a beautiful young man that they hoped to be able to sell him for a handsome price in the slave market.

However, the god saved himself by immobiliz-ing the ship in mid-ocean and causing vines and ivies to spring up and cover the hull and decks and an ivy to twine to the top of the mast.

The terrified sailors all jumped overboard and were turned into dolphins while Dionysus sum-moned his panther-drawn chariot to carry him across the waves to safety.

In Rome, ivy was a symbol of intellectual achievement. Maecenas, the wealthy and cultivat-ed patron of the the poet Horace, drew this com-pliment from his protégé:

ABOVE *Ivy pro-vides a stylized decorative motif on a Greek vase. The central figure carries two ivy wands.*

RIGHT *A deco-ration of ivy leaves and berries on a Greek bowl, illustrated in* Simplification of Natural Forms *by Lewis F. Day (1896).*

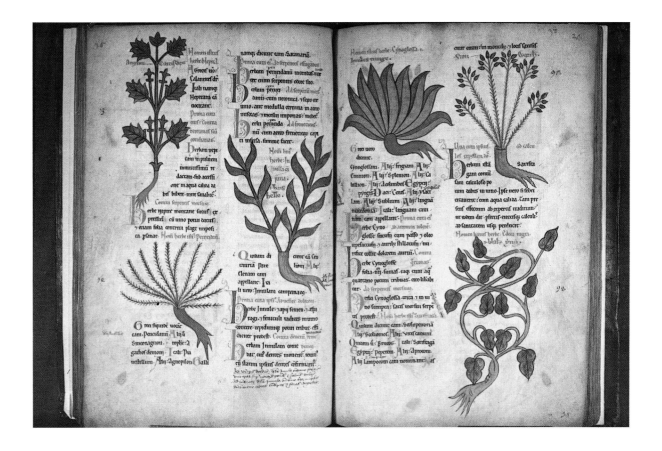

An ivy wreath, fair learning's prize
Raises Maecenas to the skies.

The vinous connotations of ivy lasted into the Middle Ages, when a bunch of ivy would be hung at the door of a tavern to advertise its wares. It was known as a bush (giving rise to the proverb 'Good wine needs no bush') or an alestake. The Summoner in Chaucer's *Canterbury Tales* had 'A garland . . . sette upon his hede, as gret as it were for an Alestake'.

In the Middle Ages ivy was thought to possess a more sinister property as a test of witchcraft. Confrontation with a cross made of ivy was supposed to make a witch reveal herself. The connection between witchcraft and ivy is also illustrated in the Legend of the Green Lady of Caerphilly in Wales. This fascinating but sinister siren was said to lure unwary travellers to their death in the middle of the night; at daybreak she would cling to the nearest wall and disappear from view, being transformed into an ivy.

DOMESTIC USES OF IVY

Some traditional theories about ivy are on the borderline between folklore and practical usefulness. According to Pliny it was commonly used as a preventive against drunkenness, and from classical times on it was prescribed as a hangover cure. If Pliny was right, the wise party-goer who took his ivy infusion before setting out for the orgy would not need it afterwards.

Homer mentions libations to the gods poured from cups of ivy wood and a later superstition that the efficacy of medicines was increased if they were drunk from an ivy wood cup, endured well into the Middle Ages. Another equally folkloric remedy, a poultice of ivy leaves steeped in vinegar as a cure for corns, is still recommended on South Uist in the Outer Hebrides.

Ivy has a prominent place in the history of herbal medicine. The seeds were a useful purgative, and an extract from the leaves and branches

Ivy (Hedera helix 'Nigra') illustrated in a 13th-century Herbal.

13

Ivy leaf decoration is the most common form of decoration in the borders of medieval manuscripts made in France and the Netherlands from c.1380 to c.1480. The ivy leaves themselves are usually executed in highly burnished gold on spiralling tendril stems and are often interspersed with little flowers, acanthus leaves and fruit. This example is of the Annunciation from the Book of Hours *by the Master of Guilebert de Mets (Southern Netherlands, c.1430–50), Sothebys, London.*

was used in the treatment of catarrh, coughs and asthma; abscesses, burns, bruises and skin rashes; haemorrhoids; and arthritis and rheumatism. John Gerard in his *Herball,* published in 1597, recommended it against smarting eyes. But today's herbalists use ivy mainly in cosmetics. Creams and lotions containing ivy extracts are also used to relieve sunburn, for massage in the treatment of cellulitis, and to refresh tired feet. An ivy bath is said to have a stimulating effect.

In *The Complete Book of Herbs,* Lesley Bremness gives this recipe for Ivy Cellulite Cream in which the effective ingredient is an ivy decoction made by simmering 2oz (50g) ivy leaves in 1pt (600ml) distilled water for 30 minutes.

2 teaspoons (10ml) beeswax
1 teaspoon (5ml) emulsifying wax
3 teaspoons (15ml) almond oil
1 teaspoon (5ml) avocado oil
4 tablespoons (60ml) double strength ivy
 decoction
8 drops each essential oils of oregano, fennel,
 rosemary

1 Melt the wax in a double boiler. Warm the oils and stir them in well.

2 Beat in the ivy decoction and allow the mixture to cool before stirring in the essential oils.

3 Spoon into a jar and label.

This massage cream is supposed to disperse trapped fluids and toxins in the fatty sub-cutaneous layers of cellulite on thighs and buttocks. Ivy can cause an allergic reaction on very sensitive skins; it is advisable to test the decoction on the skin before using it.

In the domestic sphere an ivy rinse can revitalise faded black silk, and in agriculture and horticulture too, ivy used to be valued for its practical rather than its ornamental qualities. Thomas Hill, who wrote one of the first gardening books in the sixteenth century, tells us that the Greeks used ivy bound round tree trunks to trap ants: 'by the same skilful device then, ants lodging under the shadow of these, they slay and kill'.

IVY AND THE ARTS

Distinctive foliage is a recurrent theme in the decorative arts. Ivy was used with the leaves of the lotus, vine and palm to embellish the columns of Egyptian tombs, and with the acanthus on Greek, Etruscan and Roman pottery. Among the Thracian treasures discovered in Romania in the 1970s there were gold rhytons (ritual vessels for pouring libations) decorated with the leaves and fruit of ivy. Dating from the fourth century BC, the ivy decoration indicates that they were used in the cult of Dionysus (Bacchus). A greave of consummate craftsmanship was found in a tomb of the same period near Vratsa in Bulgaria. It represents the head of a woman and a gold ivy wreath rests on her silver forehead.

Ivy, symbol of everlasting life, appears twining round the page margins of medieval Books of Hours and carved into the stone of Gothic churches: it can be seen mingled with hawthorn, holly and roses on the transept doors of Chartres Cathedral.

Later, ivy became a favourite motif for wallpapers, fabrics, china and other ornaments, and is still popular today. Table linen exquisitely worked with ivy leaves is displayed in the elegant shops in and around the Piazza San Marco in Venice, and Wedgwood plates and Tiffany dinner services are decorated with the pattern 'Napoleon ivy', from the dinner service designed for Bonaparte during his exile on the island of St Helena.

A finely wrought gold ivy wreath adorning an Etruscan helmet.

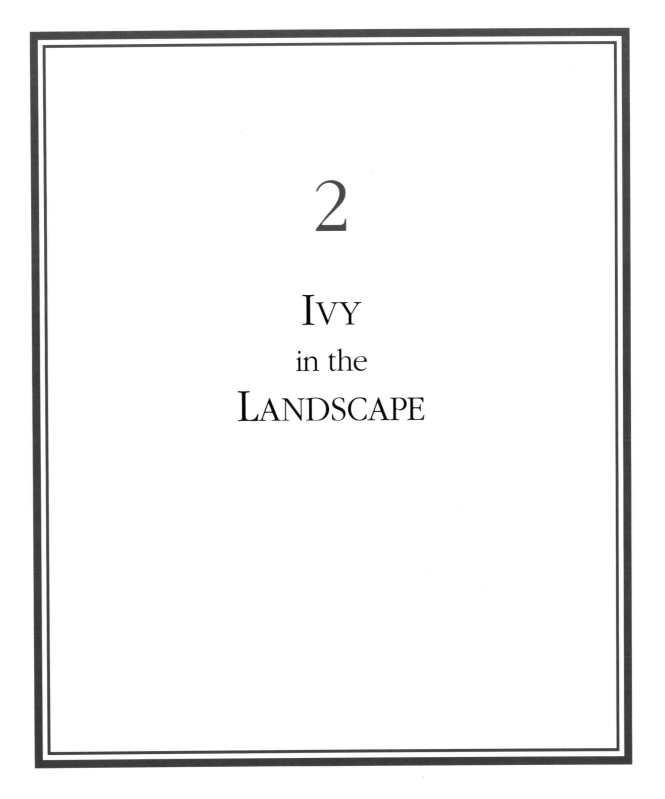

2

IVY
in the
LANDSCAPE

Ivy is such a widespread feature in the landscape that poets over the centuries have been moved to refer to it in their descriptions of nature. Euripides described:

> *The darksome, ivy-vested woods,*
> *The woods that wave o'er Ida's brow,*
> *Down whose steep sides the cool translucent*
>   *floods*
> *In many channels flow.*

The classical landscapes of ancient Greece and Rome, peopled by gods and heroes, became the favourite subjects of Poussin and Lorrain, the great seventeenth-century French painters whose work was the inspiration for the English landscape movement. Alexander Pope, the movement's poet and philosopher, described a visit he made in 1722 or 1724 to Lord Digby's house at Sherborne in Dorset: '. . . Another walk under this hill by the

riverside quite covered with high trees on both banks, overhung with ivy, where falls a natural cascade with never-ceasing murmurs.' The scene which Pope described is almost identical to Euripides' Mount Ida, and ivy adds to the poetry of both examples by cloaking the woods and river banks in mystery. In the Sherborne landscape there was also a hermit's seat of rugged stone, a ruined bridge and ruined arches. Pope approved the scene as 'inexpressibly awful and solemn'.

Natural landscapes of a gentler kind appealed to the nineteenth-century poets of the Romantic movement. Keats wrote in *Endymion*:

> *Paths there were many*
> *Winding through palmy fern, and rushes*
> * fenny*
> *And ivy banks.*

Later in the nineteenth century, the Victorians took examples from nature to express their sentimentality. In the language of flowers, ivy was deemed to express fidelity and to symbolize eternity. For this reason sprigs of ivy were often included in wedding bouquets, and ivy was used in funeral wreaths and planted on graves. Its longevity illustrated, by contrast, the ephemeral nature of man's achievements. Charles Dickens expressed that sentiment in his poem 'The Ivy Green':

> *The brave old plant in its lonely days*
> *Shall fatten upon the past,*
> *For the stateliest building man can raise*
> *Is the ivy's food at last,*
> *Creeping on where time has been,*
> *A rare old plant is the ivy green.*

Another example in the same vein comes from the Scottish poet Malcolm's *Ruins of Palmyra:*

> *The wreath that deck'd the victor's hair,*
> *Hath, like his glory, withered there;*
> *And Time's immortal garlands twine*
> *O'er Desolation's mournful shrine,*
> *Like Youth's embrace around decline.*

And plenty of worse verse was written by other hands in the Victorian era:

And still let man his fabrics wear –
August in beauty, grace, and strength,
Days pass, thou Ivy never sere,
And all is thine at length!

ABOVE *Victorian postcard*

RIGHT *An arbour partially shaded by ivy. Wood engraving by Thomas Bewick.*

OPPOSITE Hedera helix *'Goldheart' brings a touch of colour to a statue in a wintry alcove.*

A more down-to-earth approach to ivy came from the British gardening expert and writer Shirley Hibberd who did much to popularize ivy as a garden and house plant. He was born in Stepney in the East End of London in 1825, the son of a sailor who had served with Lord Nelson. A bookseller turned journalist and gardening expert, he developed a passion for foliage plants in general and for ivy in particular, and in 1872 published *The Ivy – Its History, Uses and Characteristics*. His book

was the first comprehensive survey of ivies and their uses in the garden and the house and remained the only guide for the next century. Although his great crusade was for use in the garden of the numerous varieties of ivy available by that time, he also appreciated the romantic effect of ivy in the natural landscape. The book is peppered with quotations from classical and contemporary poets and illustrated with engravings of ivy-clad church towers and castles, just as 'inexpressibly awful and solemn' as the ruins that had delighted Pope a hundred and fifty years earlier.

In France at the beginning of this century Marcel Proust also referred to the charm of ivy on old buildings. In *Within a Budding Grove* Mme de Villeparisis promises the narrator a visit to the church at Carqueville – '"Quite buried in all its old ivy," she said with a wave of the hand which seemed tastefully to be clothing the absent front in an invisible and delicate screen of foliage.'

'What should we do without ivy in the regions of the picturesque?' wrote Hibberd. 'How it marries the youth and freshness of the world to things old and crumbling to dust; how it brings the past and present into complete unity.' Sadly, today it seems that we do have to do without it in many of the situations where our ancestors found it inspirational. Throughout Europe, ruined castles and picturesque buildings have been stripped bare and scrubbed spic-and-span, and it is only in early engravings and in poetry that the romantic

Ground-cover ivy softens the edges of a stepped path in woodland.

grandeur of massive, weathered stonework clothed in ivy can still be found.

The ruthless zeal with which ancient buildings and their surroundings have been cleaned up certainly makes them more easily accessible to tourists, but at the same time it has robbed the poetic soul of inspiration and destroyed the safe haven of the 'moping owl' of Gray's *Elegy*, and of many other wild creatures.

IVY IN THE RURAL LANDSCAPE

Although most of our old buildings have been purged of it, ivy's indestructible nature still guarantees it a permanent place in the countryside. One of the pleasures of a winter walk in woodland or along hedgerows is the search for variations on the theme of native ivy. An intriguing characteristic of *Hedera helix* is its variability. A dozen leaves gathered on a short walk will each display a different shape and colour, particularly after plants have been touched by the first hard frost of the year, for many of the leaves change colour from green to blackish or reddish bronze, and the veining becomes paler and more pronounced. Although such winter colour-change is said by some authorities to be more pronounced on limestone and chalk than on acid soils, I have found it to be more a question of the severity of the frost than of the alkalinity of the soil.

The leaves of wild ivy vary in shape from the typical, broad, three-pointed leaf which artists and designers have found so appealing over the cen-

Some ivies develop winter colour in a range from pinkish-red to blackish-purple.

23

turies, to smaller leaves with delicately tapering fingers, and others resembling smooth-margined hearts. In dense shade leaves are sometimes several inches broad and long, spaced out at wide intervals on long, smooth green stems; they have adapted in order to absorb energy from the dim light that penetrates the shadows of the woodland. On ivies growing in full sun and poor, stony soil, the leaves can be tiny, dark and tough textured, and they are densely crowded on gnarled, grey woody stems.

In woodland, particularly at the margins where the wood meets meadow or cornfield, and along walks and rides, ivy forms dense ground cover, suppressing unfriendly brambles but allowing bluebells, wood anemones and primroses to grow through it in spring, a beautiful natural combination that is easily adaptable to the garden. In the

Ground-cover ivy catches the light in a woodland glade at Nymans, West Sussex.

woods ivy also scrambles upward; on some trees young ivy shoots press their neat, symmetrically arranged little leaves close to the trunks at eye level. These new leaves are a fresh and tender shade of the palest green. At the top of other trees ivy in its adult form burgeons into great, loose mops of dark foliage half-hidden by clusters of flowers or berries.

In the garden I would never deliberately plant ivy on a tree. One of the pleasures of the winter garden is the bark of trees with its varied colours and textures, and I prefer to leave it bare. However, a hedge or bank of ivy can provide the perfect background for the trunks of some trees. In the bleakest months of the year I have seen a group of birch trees thrown into relief by the sombre dark green of an ivy hedge so that they gleamed with a whiteness that made the surrounding snow seem

almost dingy. When wild ivy arrives uninvited in the garden and starts to climb a tree I allow it to remain if it has an unusual leaf shape or colour. There is one such happy accident in my garden which has climbed about 6ft (1.8m) up an ash tree – in cold weather the leaves are purplish maroon with bands of the palest lime-green following the veins. Such happy accidents are the rewards of a policy of *laissez-faire*.

Excessive tidiness in the garden – and in the landscape – can be a mistake. In many areas, the removal of hedgerows in the interests of more efficient farming, and the ruthless trimming of existing hedges, has led to the loss of habitats for wildlife and plants. This is not a new problem. In 1870 William Robinson, one of the first advocates of a natural style of gardening, commented in his book *The Wild Garden,* 'The constant clipping of

fences [for fences read hedges] is needless in many grazing and woody districts . . . where fields are large the fence should also be a shelter – a bold, free-growing screen, with Bramble, wild Rose, Ferns, Ivy, and other scrambling things that like to live in it . . . The Ivy runs through such fences and makes them very pretty, tying them together with its graceful lace work, and its growth seldom chokes the Quick or other plants.' The hedgerows which appealed to Robinson are becoming increasingly rare today. Modern machinery does the job of hedge-trimming speedily and efficiently, but the results are suitable for the boundaries of a well-kept suburban garden than for a traditional feature of the rural landscape.

The ideal country hedge should be allowed to grow tall and bushy so that it foams with hawthorn and elder blossom in summer, is laden

Leaves and berries of the adult (arborescent) Hedera helix on a frosty morning.

St Enoch's Shopping Centre, Glasgow, Scotland: one of the world's largest glass buildings.

with berries, nuts, hips and haws in autumn and in winter takes on the green and bronze hues of ivy, studded with the bloomy blue-black of its fruit.

IVY IN THE URBAN LANDSCAPE

Landscape architects who choose plants for the public landscapes of city centres and parks, industrial premises, roads and railways owe much to the ivy. It needs little maintenance and its ability to tolerate drought and air pollution makes it the only plant that will grow at all in some unpromising situations. The more robust, large-leaved, hardy varieties, such as *Hedera colchica* 'Dentata', its variegated form *H. colchica* 'Dentata Variegata' and *Hedera helix* 'Hibernica' (known as Irish ivy and sometimes, confusingly and mistakenly,

as English ivy) will quickly form a dense low ground cover on banks or level areas and will survive being walked on occasionally. These ivies will also cover a 10ft (3m) wall in just a few years.

The use of ivy for such purposes is not new. In 1868 M. Delchevalerie, whose position as *Chef de la Culture au Fleuriste* in the city of Paris must have presented him with much the same problems that those responsible for municipal planting face today, recommended in *La Belgique Horticole* the use of *le Lierre d'Irland* (Irish ivy) to cover banks and large beds. A century earlier on the other side of the Atlantic, the traveller Peter Kalm noticed near Philadelphia 'an ivy of *Hedera helix,* planted against the wall of a stone building which was so covered by the fine green leaves of this plant as almost to conceal the whole' *(Travels in North America,* 1748). This may well be the same plant described in 1844 as 'One of the most beautiful growths of this plant, which has ever met our eyes . . . that upon the old mansion in the Botanic Gardens in Philadelphia.' This was written by Andrew Jackson Downing, the great pioneer of landscape architecture, in his *Treatise on the Theory and Practice of Gardening adapted to North America.*

These tributes to ivy were made when relatively few varieties were available. In 1770 Richard Weston in *The Universal Botanist and Nurseryman* listed just four ivies, one of which was the rare yellow-berried type. By 1867, the British nurseryman, William Paul, offered 'more than forty sorts' in *The Gardener's Chronicle,* indicating that the enthusiasm for ivy as a garden plant, which Shirley Hibberd was to foster with his book *The Ivy* five years later, had already begun.

Today, there are nurseries specializing in ivies throughout the world and some offer more than 100 varieties of ivy for different purposes. Most wholesale nurseries, which are the main source of supply for landscape architects dealing with large-scale projects, still list fewer than half a dozen, but that is no reason why designers should not be more adventurous with the ivies that they specify. If they were to insist on a greater variety, demand would soon generate supply.

It is sad but true that a great many modern buildings present an unattractive face to the world. They provide an opportunity to introduce much-needed plant life into the dreariest areas of our cities. Blank facades of stained concrete or crudely coloured brick would benefit from a mantle of evergreen foliage, which would not only hide their ugliness but positively enhance them. On those dismal city walls that are covered in crude graffiti, the ill-spelt, predictable messages could be obscured by tapestries of green and variegated ivies.

Useful as ivy is to disguise ugliness in the urban environment, it also has great potential for a more positive use. Fine buildings are enhanced when their outstanding features are framed with ivy trained and clipped to make green architecture, and some of the best modern buildings are designed so that trailing ivies can cascade over roofs, balconies and window-boxes. Other buildings look splendid rising out of a sea of ivy planted at their base. Co-operation between architects and landscapers at the earliest stage of design is the exception rather than the rule, but if it became the norm, many new ways of achieving harmony between buildings and plants could be found.

Suitable ivies for landscape use include: for ground cover, *H. algeriensis*, *H. colchica* varieties, *H. Helix* 'Dragon Claw', 'Green Ripple', 'Parsley Crested' and *H. helix hibernica* 'Hamilton'. For covering walls and buildings, choose from *H. azorica, H. canariensis* 'Gloire de Marengo', *H. helix* 'Atropurpurea', 'Dragon Claw', 'Gold heart', 'Succinata', *H. helix hibernica* 'Variegata', and *H. pastuchovii*. See also Ivy Chart, pp. 111–153.

Variegated ivy softens the 1960s concrete architecture surround of the School of African and Oriental Studies building, London University.

27

3

IVIES
in the
GARDEN

---

the vertical dimension

In the 1870s, Shirley Hibberd did horticulture a great service by collecting and describing a large number of ivies, but he also caused great confusion by his esoteric approach to naming them. Experts have been clearing up the muddle ever since, but fresh problems arise because of the ease with which ivies sport or mutate. 'New' varieties that scarcely differ one from another are being discovered, named and offered commercially in different parts of the world. A British nursery, for example, may list an ivy imported from the USA under one name and its twin from the Netherlands under a completely different label. The tangle of names, synonyms and look-alike varieties is gradually being unravelled by the American Ivy Society which is the International Register for the genus *Hedera*. The names authenticated by this organization have been used in this book as far as possible; where a more familiar, long-established popular name also exists, both have been given.

More than 400 different ivy varieties are in cultivation; most are undamaged by severe frosts, others are better grown as house plants; some ivies climb and scramble, others are ideal as ground cover. The chart starting on page 114 lists in alphabetical order all ivies, with their synonyms and look-alikes, currently available from specialist nurseries. It describes each plant's characteristics, its hardiness, rate of growth, suitable site and potential uses.

IVIES FOR WALLS

One of ivy's great virtues is that it actually *likes* a north wall. There are several good climbing plants that will tolerate such a position, but precious few that will revel in it. Shirley Hibberd wrote that ivies 'grow more luxuriantly, and acquire finer colours, on a damp wall facing north than in any other situation or aspect'. Exceptions to this are the yellow-leaved variety 'Buttercup', and ivies with yellow variegations, such as 'Goldheart'. These need plenty of light to bring out their colour, although the leaves will scorch if they are in a very hot, dry

PREVIOUS PAGE *Ivy and alchemilla mollis by a garden fountain in Rosemary Verey's garden at Barnsley House, Gloucestershire.*

ABOVE *A garden of quietly contrasting foliage with ivies as climbers and ground cover.*

The best of evergreen climbers is our native Ivy, and the many beautiful forms allied to it or that have arisen from it. Ivy in our woods arranges its own beautiful effects, but in gardens it might be made more delightful use of . . . for edgings, banks, forming screens, covering old trees, and forming summerhouses . . ., ivy-covered wigwams . . . and covered ways. . . A bower of one of the handsome-leaved Ivies in a grove of Box would be charming, and its charms would last long.
William Robinson, *The Wild Garden* (1870)

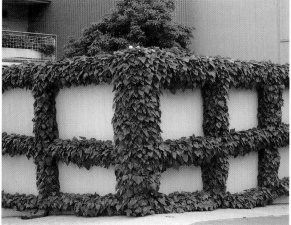

position. So they are happiest on an east or west-facing wall where they will get plenty of light but will not receive the full blast of the midday sun. In any case, most gardeners will want to reserve the prime position of a south-facing wall for more demanding climbers that will not thrive elsewhere rather than waste it on an ivy which will be perfectly happy in a humbler place.

Ivy's self-clinging propensity is another great advantage. Most other climbing plants need to be tied to supports at regular intervals, or they will get out of hand. If they are to achieve any great height, tying in new growth involves hair-raising

ABOVE Hedera helix *'Goldheart' trained on wires to form a living diagonal trellis.*

LEFT *A bold square pattern of ivy in stark contrast to a white balcony wall.*

31

A foliage group of contrasting colour and texture in Margery Fish's garden at East Lambrook Manor: Hedera helix *'Buttercup',* Euphorbia Wulfenii, Alchemilla mollis *and* Geranium endressii.

feeding and watering, the plant will soon put out vigorous new shoots, and after a few years will be as good as ever.

Ivy's qualities as a climber have long been appreciated. The description in Gerard's *Herball* (1597) says, 'It cleaveth wonderfull hard upon trees, and upon the smoothest stone walls.' Ivy will not damage a healthy tree or a sound wall. On the contrary, on the walls of buildings it has the advantage of providing good insulation, keeping damp out and warmth in. It can embellish a handsome stone or brick wall, or disguise one of ugly concrete or breeze blocks.

Ivy is an unrivalled disguise for eyesores, but it can also be used to enhance fine buildings. Closely clipped to frame arches and pediments, it becomes an integral part of the architecture. On a grand, classical building, the large-leaved varieties provide the right scale. One of the most dramatic is *Hedera colchica* 'Dentata'. A 1910 catalogue by V. N. Gauntlett and Co. Ltd, of Chiddingfold, Surrey, described it as 'the *most effective* of all ivies . . . where an evergreen climber is required *nothing can equal it'*. It does indeed provide spectacular, dense cover with huge glossy leaves of 8 x 7in (20 x 17cm), and can climb rapidly to a great height. It is hardy in most of Europe and as far north as Zone 5 in the USA. I would choose to grow this against a large expanse of stone. The equally hardy, variegated clone, *Hedera colchica* 'Dentata Variegata' has grey-green leaves with creamy-yellow margins and provides a wonderful contrast against red brick. It has the advantage, too, of not scorching in strong sunlight. The colouring of 'Dentata Variegata' is reversed in another good Colchica ivy, with slightly smaller leaves, 'Sulphur Heart'; also known as 'Paddy's Pride' or 'Gold Leaf', it carries the yellow variegation in splashes and streaks on the centre of the leaves.

work from the top of a stepladder with a recalcitrant branch in one hand, secateurs in the other, and string between your teeth. Daunting if you have a poor head for heights, and impossible to yell for help.

Sooner or later the problem also arises of how to deal with climbers when the wall needs painting or re-pointing. With ivy the plant can simply be cut down to near the base and all the growth pulled away from the wall. It means sacrificing the cover it has produced over the years, but, with

Where space does not permit such grand effects, there is a wide choice of green and variegated ivies, displaying enormous diversity of leaf shapes and sizes. It is worth visiting a specialist nursery to compare characteristics and outstanding features. All ivies are reliably hardy plants in

all but the harshest climates. Some will suffer damage to the leaves from sharp, cold winds and can look a sorry sight in winter, but most recover with the return of milder weather. In areas of very hard frosts, all top growth may be killed, but shoots will appear from the base in spring if the dead material is cut back.

Ivies with yellow or cream variegation can bring an effect of dappled sunlight to a dark wall, such as one often finds enclosing a dingy, narrow passage at the side of a semi-detached town house.

Seen from a distance, a wall covered in variegated ivy can even give the illusion that it is covered in yellow or white flowers.

Of all ivies with yellow variegations, *Hedera helix* 'Goldheart' is the most striking. This is such a successful plant that it runs the risk of being despised for its popularity. I have heard garden snobs murmur disapprovingly of its vulgarity, a fate which often befalls those plants which are to be seen in every garden. However, no garden should be without 'Goldheart' – it is quite the most

A tool shed completely smothered in ivy in a cottage garden in Oxfordshire.

cheerful sight throughout the winter months. The stems cling close and branch prettily against a wall, and the leaves – of typical ivy shape – retain pure, clear yellow centres set off by dark green margins. It is essentially a wall plant as the growth is too sparse for ground cover and the trails do not hang well from containers.

'Buttercup' is the only ivy with leaves that are consistently yellow all over, and much sought after for that reason. But it needs a wall to maintain its colour, and plenty of light; in shade or when used as ground cover, it does not colour well, the leaves remaining a disappointing pale green. A young plant of 'Buttercup' straight from the nursery will have green leaves, too, but they will colour up as the plant develops. Like all yellow-leaved plants, it shows to greatest advantage when contrasted with dark green foliage and makes a good contrast with red or purple flowers,

such as Clematis 'Jackmanii', for example, or the climbing rose 'Veilchenblau'.

There are not many hardy climbing ivies with pure white variegations – most tend to be creamy. *Hedera canariensis* 'Gloire de Marengo' is a handsome and fast-growing exception. It has large leaves of green mixed with silver-grey, with white at the margins, especially on young leaves. It is not cheerful in a hard winter, as ivy ought to be, because severe weather causes it to lose many of its leaves. I also like the soft, silvery markings of *Hedera helix* 'Glacier' which is said to be hardy in USA Zone 7, and, for tidier leaves with a more pronounced and regular white variegation at the margins, I would choose 'Adam'. It is usually recommended for pots or hanging baskets, but will climb a wall happily, is reliably hardy and tidy of growth, and as a bonus the leaves sometimes turn pink at the edges in cold weather.

Hedera helix *in a natural-looking group with* Clematis x durandii *and a wineberry in Rosemary Verey's garden at Barnsley House, Gloucestershire.*

For very inhospitable sites there is nothing to beat the ordinary English ivy, *Hedera helix*. It will grow almost anywhere provided the soil is not waterlogged. The brilliant garden designer Russell Page, faced in France with a problem wall 100ft (30m) long and 20ft (6m) high, north-facing with heavy, wet, limy soil at its base, chose to clothe it with common ivy. This formed the backdrop for a planting scheme which depended for interest entirely on the different textures and shades of evergreen leaves. In front of the wall he planted alternating bushes of *Viburnum rhytidophyllum* and *Aucuba japonica,* with large-leaved Handsworth box and a carpet of bergenia in front. Russell Page wrote of this successful scheme, 'These are the most ordinary of plants and the

whole effect of this planting, all dark green, comes from the different way each species reflects or absorbs the light.' It would be interesting to devise a similar scheme using only ivies with leaves of different sizes and textures, as climbers and shrubs, on pillars and as ground cover.

Plain, green ivy forms a good background to colourful flowering plants. In her book published in 1862, *Flower and Fruit Decoration,* T. C. Marsh gives suggestions for a city garden. Her book was mainly about flower arranging and table decorations, but she also showed diagrams of brightly coloured bedding schemes. To set them off she said one should 'Cover the walls entirely with ivy planted all round at intervals of two feet . . . the best is the large Irish ivy . . . seen to perfection in the long wall by Constitution Hill which separates Green Park from Buckingham Palace gardens.' Many city gardens today would benefit from this treatment, particularly in cities where an industrial legacy has left dismal brick walls with the appearance of having absorbed centuries of soot. The rickety trellis which is often seen adding a few extra feet of height to such walls would also be improved by a dense, green covering.

Other ivies that display their qualities well against walls include *H. helix* 'Angularis Aurea', 'Cavendishii', 'Eva', 'Fleur de Lis', 'Glymii', 'Mrs Pollock', 'Pedata', 'Succinata', 'Tess'; *H. helix hibernica* 'Variegata', *H. nepalensis* and *H. pastuchovii.* See also Ivy Chart, pp. 111 – 153.

HEDGES AND FENCES

The treatment of boundaries and divisions within gardens is often a problem. Attractive walls and fences are expensive to construct and good evergreen hedges, such as yew or holly, take many years to grow tall enough to fulfil their purpose. In small gardens you would also need to sacrifice precious planting space to a minimum width of 3ft (90cm) in order to accommodate a good hedge.

Ivy can provide an excellent alternative, making an attractive barrier in a short time, of 6ft (1.8m) or so in height yet no more than 1ft (30cm) wide.

This idea dates from the nineteenth century and deserves to be revived. Ivy hedges were recommended in Cassell's *Popular Gardening* in the 1870s as 'Elegant and very effective screens, which do not take up a quarter the space a hedge would require'. Support for the ivy can be built from single courses of breeze blocks or, even simpler, of split-chestnut palings or wire chain-link fencing fixed to angle-iron supports. Unappealing but cheap, in each case. To hide the support fence as quickly as possible, plant the fastest-growing kinds of ivy 1ft (30cm) apart. Tying the shoots to the support will help them along in the right direction, and, once they have reached the top, the hedge should be clipped over twice a year. *Hedera colchica* 'Dentata', *H. helix* 'Digitata', 'Dragon Claw', 'Glymii' which becomes purplish with white veins in winter, 'Green Ripple', 'Hibernica', or 'Trustee' are all green-leaved varieties which will do the job of hedging well and make a good

Cool ivies form both background and foreground to the hot reds of Alstroemerias.

A Renaissance stone lion crouches on an ivy pedestal in the garden of the castle at Gourdon, Côte d'Azur.

background for other plants. If the hedge is to be a feature in its own right, rather than a background, a tapestry effect can be achieved by planting a mixture of plain and variegated kinds. Ivies can also be introduced at the base of existing evergreen or deciduous hedges for a tapestry effect.

The quickest way to thicken up a neglected hedge that has become gappy and scrawny is to plant a dense, bushy kind of ivy in the gaps: common English ivy, 'Brokamp' or 'Shamrock', would be suitable. In a country hedge, native ivy will probably arrive of its own accord. There is plenty in a mixed hedge on the boundary of my garden in the Cotswolds, and in winter when the hawthorn, blackthorn and field maple are without leaves, the ivy, which has reached its arborescent form, gives colour all autumn and winter, not only from the leaves but also from the flowers which,

although generally described as insignificant, cover the hedge with a greeny-gold haze, and later from the berries in rounded bunches which change from pale green to blue-black. Arborescent ivy can be planted to make an excellent self-supporting hedge, evergreen and with the bonus of flowers and fruit.

PILLARS, PERGOLAS AND PAVILIONS

'A green thought in a green shade' under an arbour of ivy might be just the refreshment the gardener needs on a hot summer's day. Ivy has long been valued in Mediterranean countries as a provider of cool retreats from the heat of the sun. In the past it has been used to clothe garden structures from rudimentary rustic timber frameworks to elaborate and fantastic trellised pavilions. An illustration in Jacques Androuet du Cerceau's *Les Plus Excellents Batiments de France* (1576 and 1579) shows the *pièce de résistance* of the gardens at Montargis. This is a magnificent Renaissance gallery with three arched, pedimented and domed pavilions. The entire, majestic structure is built in 'carpenter's work', and du Cerceau reported that the structure was 'now covered in ivy'.

Ivy is hard to beat for relatively instant green architecture. Since it will soon be covered, the supporting structure can be quite rough and ready, made from larch poles or stout bamboo canes securely lashed together. If something more elegant is wanted, ready-made metal arches or arbours can be used. By fixing wire netting to the framework, an enclosed ivy summerhouse can be constructed, with spaces left for doors and windows. Once the ivy cover is established, roses and clematis can be grown up the green walls. Existing garden buildings can sometimes benefit from the discreet use of ivy to partly conceal and partly reveal their charms.

Newly erected summerhouses, gazebos, balustrades or even ruins of stone (real or fake) can look raw for several years while one waits for algae and lichen to provide the desired antique patina. The Romans trained ivy up pillars at Pompeii, and if we follow their example, new structures can be quickly and naturally assimilated into the garden landscape. This applies equally to statuary, urns and even to stone furniture. A piece strategically placed as a focal point or to close a vista will look less contrived if a few graceful tendrils are allowed to creep over it from a clump of ivy at the base. The effect to be aimed at can be seen in Italian gardens, where greenery and stonework have been combined happily for centuries. The tradition was already alive when Cicero was left in charge of work on the garden at his brother's villa. He wrote to him that everything was looking 'marvellously pleasant with a fishpond, spouting fountains, an open space and plantation. Your gardener has clothed everything with ivy . . . so that your Greek statues seem to have been turned into gardeners selling ivy.'

The contrast between light and shade is impor-

tant in gardens, and can be experienced by moving from open sunlight to enclosed greenery. An ivy tunnel can effectively define the transition from one part of the garden to another area of different character, adding a sense of mystery. It might be planted with alternate green and variegated ivies and should lead from an area full of stimulating flower-colour to a restful, leafy enclosure where the main attractions are mossy rocks, ferns and the intriguing miniature shrubby ivies 'Congesta', 'Erecta' and 'Conglomerata'. They are

An ivy-smothered urn behind an 18th-century statue of Pomona.

not beautiful but are interesting for their form and growth habit. Some gardeners consider their slightly contorted, dwarfish form freakish, but I think they have great charm. The focal point in this green enclosure might be a dripping grotto, covered and surrounded by those ivies which display unusual leaf shapes, such as 'Parsley Crested', 'Pedata' and 'Ivalace'. It would evoke Tennyson's poem, 'The Lotus-Eaters':

Here are cool mosses deep,
And thro the moss the ivies creep,
And in the stream the long-leaved flowers
*   weep,*
And from the craggy ledge the poppy hangs in
*   sleep.*

In more formal parts of the garden ivy trained on tunnels or pergolas forms an excellent background to roses, clematis or vines, and ensures that the structure remains ornamental in the winter months, when flowers have faded and leaves fallen. Where shade limits the choice of plants, as is so often the case in small town gardens, ivies are invaluable for providing vertical accents in borders or as part of a formal pattern. They can be trained to poles or to simple timber or metal structures to make square or round pillars, arches or umbrellas, and according to which ivy you choose, their style can be elegant or robust.

Green and variegated ivies can also be trained or grafted to form mop-headed or weeping standards (see chapter 9 for grafting method), to give height in a border or to mark the centre and corners of knot garden beds. All ivies, except the shrubby types and those that are grown in the arborescent or adult form, will climb, but some are slower than others. Some will make a delicate open tracery on a wall or fence, while others will achieve a dense cover.

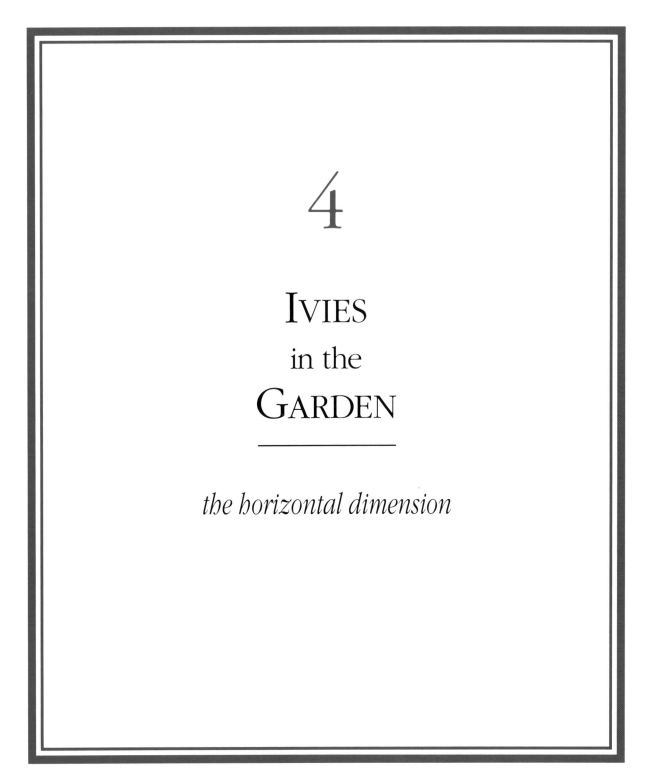

4

Ivies
in the
Garden

---

the horizontal dimension

PREVIOUS PAGE
At Meadowbrook Farm, Pennsylvania, ivies are used for topiary in the urns and to soften the base of the steps.

ABOVE *A broad, winding sweep of* Hedera helix *'Glacier'.*

Landscape architects know the value of ivy as a rapidly established, weed-smothering evergreen ground cover for shaded areas. It is ideal for public places as it requires little maintenance, and will stand being walked on in moderation. Gardeners are less aware of its potential. The more colourful and unusual ivies are popular as house plants, but many people do not realize that most varieties which are sold for indoor use are robust enough for the garden. Margery Fish, who did much to make the cottage style of gardening popular, made imaginative use of such ivies in her garden at East Lambrook Manor in Somerset. In her book *Ground Cover Plants* (1964) she wrote: 'Whenever I go to a function where house plants are given as presents to the ladies I inevitably choose a variegated ivy, and just as inevitably I plant the ivy as ground cover the moment I get home.' The majority of her free acquisitions seem to have thrived.

If you plan to transfer an ivy that has been

grown indoors or in a greenhouse to an outdoor site, it is best to plant it out in late spring or early summer when the climate outside is similar to that indoors.

IVIES AS GROUND COVER

Most gardens have areas where maintenance is a problem and where grass does not provide effective cover: obstacles which are too large to remove, such as tree stumps or rocks; low retaining walls that are poorly built or have collapsed; banks which are too steep or too stony to mow; ground beneath trees or between large shrubs where grass is depressingly sparse.

These are the places for bold sweeps of *Hedera colchica, H. canariensis,* or *H. helix* 'Hibernica', in either their green or variegated forms. Planted under trees, they know their place and, unlike the common ivy, will not make a nuisance of themselves by climbing a tree when your back is turned. *H. canariensis* is less hardy than the other two so it needs a position where winter winds cannot blast it. On the ground these three can be planted 3ft (1m) apart although landscapers wanting quick results prefer a closer planting distance of 2ft (60cm). These ivies will spread quite rapidly to form a level sward about 1ft (30cm) high, each plant covering some 100 sq ft (9 sq m).

Good examples of 'Hibernica' used in this way can be seen in large-scale landscaping in many cities in North America and in Northern Europe. It is also used to good effect in the National Trust's gardens of Nymans in Sussex, Anglesey Abbey in Cambridgeshire and in the Royal Botanic Gardens at Kew, Surrey, all of which can be visited. 'Hibernica' and *H. colchica* 'Dentata', with its two var-

Ivy used in a knot garden at the USA National Arboretum, Washington DC.

Trees rise out of a sea of Hedera helix 'Hibernica' at the National Trust's Anglesey Abbey, Cambridgeshire.

iegated clones 'Dentata Variegata' and 'Sulphur Heart', are also landscapers' favourites for providing handsome ground cover in public spaces in cities throughout the temperate world. They are equally useful in private gardens where comparatively large areas need to be covered. To start the plants off well, spread the shoots out and peg them down or weight them to encourage them to root. Growing tips can be pinched out to induce side-branching. The plants are easily restrained by clipping when they have filled their allotted space. Ivies with unusual leaves that make good ground cover include 'Dragon Claw', 'Parsley Crested' and 'Pin Oak' which has small pointed light green leaves and, although it has the delicate appearance of a miniature ivy, will quickly form tidy mounds of cover.

The convert to ivy will want to grow it not just in order to solve gardening problems, but for its own sake. In most gardens space is at a premium, so positions must be found for ivy where it can co-exist with other plants. The relatively compact varieties are obliging in this respect; grown beneath trees and shrubs, they will allow bulbs and other foliage plants to push up through their leaves in the due season, while at the same time preventing weed seeds from germinating. When flowering plants put on their display, ivies form a complementary background. Later, when the branches of shrubs and trees are bare, and the foliage of bulbs and herbaceous plants has disappeared, the ivies become the stars of the show.

The range of ivies suitable for ground-cover planting was greatly increased in the 1920s when Paul Randolph of Verona, Pennsylvania, discovered a sport from one of his ivies which revolutionized ivy breeding. He called it 'Pittsburgh', and, together with many virtually indistinguishable clones, such as 'Chicago', 'Hahn Self-Branching', 'Ray's Supreme' and 'Spitzberg', it is still available today, usually being marketed as a house plant. The valuable characteristic of 'Pittsburgh' is its short-jointed, self-branching habit, which makes a dense, compact plant. It has small, mid-green leaves, but is the ancestor of most of the variegated ivies available today, and of many of those with weird and wonderful leaf shapes.

The choice of ground-cover ivies for the garden is limited only by their ability to resist bad weather, and by the effect required. Most ivies are frost-hardy, but some of those with delicate variegated leaves are damaged and look scruffy in cold wet weather. Certain of the small-leaved varieties of delicate appearance but robust constitution are ideal as carpeting plants through which spring bulbs can grow. The soft, light green leaves of 'Direktor Badke' are small, rounded and set close together on the stems; it would make a pretty foil to dwarf narcissi. At Barnsley House in Gloucestershire, Rosemary Verey has planted snowdrops to grow through 'Luzii', and the soft grey-green leaves of this ivy, blotched and speckled with yellow, blend well with the snowdrops' glaucous leaves. 'Glacier' is also a pretty companion for snowdrops.

The cream variegation of the fingered leaves of 'Sagittifolia Variegata' will lighten a shady corner of the garden and set off the purple flowers of *Iris reticulata* or dark blue crocuses very early in the year. It suffers less from frost damage than some of the variegated forms whose leaves are browned by desiccating winter winds. However, all ivies are tougher than is generally believed. Margery Fish celebrated their robust constitution when she wrote in *Ground Cover Plants,* 'The only cheerful things in my garden one awful winter were the variegated ivies, and that year Somerset was as hard hit as anywhere. When everything else was frozen to ramrods, desiccated by intense cold and seared by unceasing bitter winds, the ivies remained sleek and untouched . . . when the snow went at last the ivies I use to cover the ground under trees and on banks were just as good as before the winter.'

Among the variegated ivies that Mrs Fish grew she prized 'Harold' as the most generous. It is still available, correctly spelt 'Harald', and has medium-sized, shiny green and yellow leaves, paling to cream as the leaves age. She praised 'Tricolor', 'Heise', 'Luzii' and 'Glacier'. She also recommended 'Marmorata', one of those ivies with a name problem: it is similar to 'Luzii', 'Masquerade' and 'Gold Dust', and its dark green leaves, brushed

Hedera helix 'Sagittifolia Variegata': an elegant ground cover to lighten dark corners.

Plain green ivy as ground cover in a garden of restrained formality at Pepsico, NY.

with lime, are speckled with yellow, narrowly avoiding the virus-ridden look of some of the spotty varieties.

The advantage of growing bulbs through ivies is that the dying foliage of the bulbs is, to a great extent, concealed by the ivy. Tulips look good grown in this way, either in big, informal clumps among shrubs or in borders, or formally regimented where ivy is used as a broad edging to a bed or as infill for a knot or parterre. 'Black Parrot' and

other tulips of rich, dusky colouring look splendidly exotic with cream variegated ivies; soft pink tulips will prolong the bulb season when planted to follow the snowdrops in a carpet of 'Glacier'; tulips with yellow or white flowers associate well with yellow-splashed or dappled ivies, and scarlets and crimsons with those ivies which have fresh green leaves. In formal schemes plain green ivies provide the right lush but simple background for the huge, sumptuous flowers of parrot

and paeony-flowered tulips. If alliums are planted to follow the tulips in such schemes, their globular heads are as handsome in seed as they are in flower, so that the season of interest provided by bulbs will extend from snowdrops in late winter right through to autumn.

Ivy is a useful plant to smooth the transition from garden to landscape, having, as it were, a foot in both camps, and looks appropriately natural planted at the entrance to a woodland area

with groups of lilies and Japanese anemones rising from it. In similar situations ivies offer scope for planning beautiful foliage effects in association with other plants grown primarily for their striking leaves. In shade the bold leaves of hostas offer a range of colour and variegation that can be used either to contrast with or echo the colouring of ivies. Ferns and ivies make natural companions, and *Helleborus argutifolius, H. lividus corsicus, Euphorbia characias* and Solomon's seal *(Poly-*

A compact edging of ivy contrasts with the smooth stone coping of a small lily pond.

gonatum x *hybridum)* are all the right height to bridge the gap between ground-cover ivies and taller shrubs.

A solid, uniform edging to a bed or border has the effect of unifying a planting scheme. We are used to seeing beds edged with neat, low box hedges, or sprawling lavender, but in Victorian times ivy was much used for this purpose. In 1866 the gardening magazine edited by Shirley Hibberd, *The Floral World and Garden Guide,* recommended Irish ivy ('Hibernica') as the best for edging, and an article in the same magazine a year later described a broad edging of *H. canariensis* thriving 'in a place much exposed to smoke and dust' in London. When one thinks of the Dickensian London fogs of those days, that is quite a startling tribute to the plant's ability to withstand air pollution. Both these ivies are for large-scale use. 'Glacier' with its soft grey colouring, or the curly-leaved 'Manda's Crested' (also sold as 'Curly Locks') with pink-red winter colour are equally bold choices as edging for borders of more modest dimensions. In the smallest gardens, 'Duck-foot' is the ideal choice. A compact miniature ivy with small green leaves whose shape is well described by its name, it attracted much attention when displayed as an edging in an exhibit at Chelsea Flower Show staged by Fibrex Nurseries, the British ivy specialists.

Bright variegated ivies can be used as edging plants, but care should be taken at the planning stage to make sure they do not eclipse the plants which they are intended to frame and enhance. They are more appropriately used as part of a pattern of foliage colours and textures, for example in a formal knot or parterre in the style of the sixteenth and early seventeenth centuries. There is a handsome example of variegated ivy used in this way in a garden in Colonial Williamsburg where it weaves a serpentine band between a path and a neatly clipped box hedge. If you enjoy planning the geometry of formal patterns in the garden, there are endless combinations of plain and patterned ivies to be made, using small, compact varieties. Excellent ivies for this purpose include 'Little Diamond' and 'Adam', both with white-cream markings. 'Deltoidea' (the Sweetheart Ivy), with dark green heart-shaped leaves, 'Merion Beauty' with small bright green leaves of typical ivy shape, and 'Shamrock' are all dense and tidy green ivies, and, for a golden touch, 'Hibernica Sulphurea' is exceptionally hardy, and 'Gold Craft' can be used in sheltered areas of Britain and in Zone 8 and perhaps Zone 7 in the USA.

Other good ivies for covering medium-sized areas include *H. helix* 'Brokamp', 'Deltoidea', 'Ivalace', 'Plume d'Or' and 'Sagittifolia Variegata'. For smaller areas there are 'Adam', 'Little Diamond', 'Little Gem', 'Pin Oak' and 'Shamrock'; for edging purposes good choices include 'Brokamp', 'Conglomerata' and 'Ivalace' in addition to those already mentioned. See also Ivy Chart, pp.111–153.

IVIES AS SHRUBS

In Victorian gardens it was standard practice to use ivies as specimen plants in winter bedding schemes. Tree ivies were produced from cuttings taken from plants in their adult or arborescent phase. The plant then retains its adult characteristics and grows as a flowering and fruiting shrub. Trailing ivies were sometimes grown as standards, retaining their juvenile form and growing in much the same way as a weeping standard rose does. They were produced either by grafting on to a strong, straight stem of the shrub x *Fatshedera lizei* or by training a single shoot of the ivy up a stake and eliminating side-shoots until it had reached the desired height.

Today these forms are seldom used, but they are unusual and interesting features either treated as permanent planting as an alternative to other evergreen shrubs or as temporary winter bedding plants. The range of colour and texture they can provide and their ability to tolerate shade add greatly to the beauty of the garden in winter.

For yellow foliage in winter, ivies have a purity of colour that is hard to find in other evergreen plants. There are numerous 'golden' conifers available, some of them quite fast-growing, but their colouring can be harsh. They are best combined with other, more sober plants of similar habit, and best seen from a distance (the greater the distance the better: I would prefer them to be

over the horizon!). Other yellow-leaved plants, such as the golden privet, also tend towards brassy colouring, though to a lesser extent. Looking out of my window in January I see just three plants with yellow colouring that are truly pleasing to the eye. One is the much despised spotted laurel, *Aucuba japonica* 'Variegata'. This is another plant to which distance lends enchantment; seen at close quarters the leaves are coarse and the yellow spots make the plant look diseased, but looked at across the lawn in a dark north-facing corner it seems to be touched by sunlight. *Lonicera nitida* 'Baggesen's Gold' and *Elaeagnus pungens* 'Maculata' are the other two that are pleasing. The elaeagnus is a soft, buttery yellow without the rather neon effect of its relation 'Limelight', and the lonicera's leaves give a delicate, feathery effect. *Choisya ternata* 'Sundance' seems to have great appeal to many gardeners, but I am

ABOVE LEFT *Ivy trained to form an umbrella.*

ABOVE *Ivy trained on canes to form a pyramid. Both illustrations are taken from* The Ivy *by Shirley Hibberd (1872).*

Hedera helix *'Erecta', one of the only two shrubby ivies that neither climb nor trail. They are true shrubs, not to be confused with the arborescent adult form of climbing ivies.*

sure that when the novelty wears off, its sickly, chlorotic look will send it out of fashion.

There are some hollies with pretty yellow variegations, and others with even prettier white-margined leaves, but they are very slow growing, and for the gardener impatient to improve the winter garden, standard and shrubby ivies are a more exciting prospect. The tall, weeping mound that a standard ivy will form is a shape not readily found among evergreen plants. It makes a fine

contrast of form in a mixed planting, in summer as well as winter, and also lends itself to more formal use if two plants are used to frame a flight of steps or a doorway, or if several are planted as an avenue either side of a path.

Green ivies as well as those with variegated leaves are effective grown in this way. Any of those which throw long trails will quickly develop the required shape and it is a good way to display a favourite leaf shape. 'Ivalace' has crimped and curled leaves, as has 'Parsley Crested', and both form spectacular weeping standards. 'Pedata', the bird's-foot ivy, provides a complete contrast to these: the leaves have elegant long, thin claws with prominent veins and are set quite far apart on the fast-growing stems, which adds to the grace of the plant when it is grown as a standard. The weeping habit of these standards allows the trailing stems to stir in the slightest breeze, adding a dimension of movement to the garden.

Nurseries and garden centres do not sell ivies trained in this way, but grafting is not difficult, and the method is explained in the chapter on cultivation and propagation.

The same effect can be achieved by growing three ivies of the same variety up a stout post and allowing the shoots to cascade down when they have reached the top.

Arborescent ivies are occasionally available from nurseries, though not in any great variety. The arborescent form is more difficult to propagate than the juvenile, and slow to develop. There is too little demand for these interesting plants for their production to be a commercial proposition, but some of the nurseries which specialize in ivies are prepared to propagate them to order for regular customers and collectors. Ivies of the World list in their catalogue arborescent forms of 'Cuspidata Minor', 'Tomboy', 'Poetica' and 'Cavendishii' which in its climbing form is a usefully hardy, variegated plant with cream-white margins to the leaves. The adult form retains the variegation and bears black berries in profusion. This ivy has been known since 1867 and may have been named in honour of the Duke of Devonshire, Cavendish being the family name of the Dukes of Devonshire. 'Poetica' is a rarity among ivies because its fruits are orange, and for this reason it is the arborescent form that is most sought after. Pliny in his *Natural History* (AD 23–79) described the berries as saffron-coloured and said that it was this ivy with its golden berries that was used for wreaths to honour poets, hence its name. Its history is perhaps the most attractive thing about it.

As the adult ivies flower late into the autumn and carry their fruits all through the winter, I am

sure they would be much in demand as shrubs if they were more readily available.

There is also a small group of ivies whose natural habit of growth is shrubby rather than climbing or trailing. 'Congesta' is an intriguing plant quite unlike any other ivy, or indeed any other shrub. Slow-growing and very hardy, it holds its stems stiffly upright, and numerous, symmetrically arranged small dark green leaves are held tight against the stems. Its tidy air of formality gives it great charm, but it is so unusual that it is not easy to place among other plants. It is seen at its best in the rock garden, and looks good against stone or at the base of a rough stone wall. It also makes a good and unusual edging plant. 'Erecta' is a shrub of similar habit to 'Congesta' but is a larger plant, reaching 4ft (1.2m) in height. It is also a plant of unusual architectural form, but does not have the delightfully eccentric style of 'Congesta'.

A third plant is grouped with these two; strictly speaking it is not a shrub, will not climb and does not trail. The character of 'Conglomerata' is shown to best effect if it is allowed to spread horizontally, which it will do at a snail's pace, pushing short, thick shoots upwards and outwards, each shoot bearing a dense covering of small dark green leaves, leathery and puckered. It looks right among rocks or at the top of a low wall where it can be examined close to eye level.

Hedera helix 'Ivalace': one of the best all-purpose ivies, providing excellent ground cover and an elegant trailer.

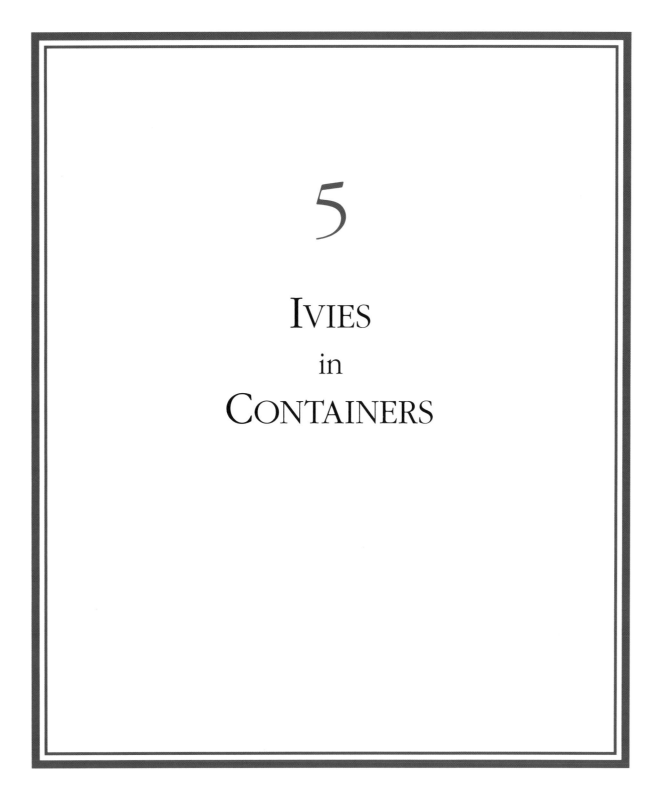

5

IVIES
in
CONTAINERS

The practice of growing plants in pots goes back a long way: at least as far as 235 BC when Hieron II, the ruler of Syracuse, decorated his garden with 'Bowers of white ivy and grapevines . . . in casks filled with earth'. Hieron II's 'white ivy' may be the first variegated form to be recorded.

Ivies are frequently grown as indoor decoration, but there are plenty of good reasons for growing these robust and elegant plants in containers outdoors as well as inside. It is obviously an advantage to be able to move plants around without having to dig them up, and when those ivies which are susceptible to frosts or desiccating winter winds are grown in containers, they can be moved inside for protection at the end of autumn. Conversely, hardy ivies are ideal for setting out in the garden as winter decoration to replace the summer display of flowers. For both purposes ivies can be grown in ornamental pots and moved around to vary the decoration of terraces, patios and roof gardens. Alternatively, ordinary plastic or clay pots of ivy can be sunk in the soil of beds and borders to give the illusion of permanence.

In extreme climates pots and tubs can be moved out of scorching sunlight at midday, or brought under cover when serious storms threaten. In drought conditions selective watering is easier.

The best reason of all for growing plants in containers is that a garden can be created without any soil and in precious little space. On a roof, balcony or window ledge ivies are ideal because of their ability to grow vertically, both upwards and downwards, as well as horizontally. The roots of most varieties need little space, and most can survive occasional neglect. Some of those ivies that suffer leaf damage from desiccating winter winds will do well if sheltered by the walls of a heated building. Composts for containers and the regime of care needed for ivies in pots and boxes are explained in chapter 9 – 'Cultivation and Propagation'.

The design of window-boxes, balconies and roof gardens can be appreciated from, quite literally, two points of view. One is the outward-looking vista from the windows of a room. The other is the view from the street or from within the roof garden. The view from the street can be enjoyed not only by the owner and by visitors, but also by the casual passer-by. It is such a pleasure to see plants growing in city streets that by 'greening' the front of your property, you will be doing the whole neighbourhood a favour. In many areas windowboxes provide the only plant life to be enjoyed, and by keeping them as luxuriant as possible at all seasons a measure of spiritual refreshment is provided. Although a few ivies in a wooden trough do not make a rain forest, they do make a small contribution to the oxygenation of city air. With some skilful green diplomacy a consortium of tenants might be persuaded to drape an entire building with foliage.

An enterprising Residents' Association could also act to provide a green cloak for the walls of that dismal well which lies at the centre of many apartment blocks. In this well, kitchen windows too often look on to the blank wall opposite. Such dreary walls can be transformed by fixing planting troughs to them with brackets at vertical intervals of about 10ft (3m). If the boxes are planted with really robust ivies such as *Hedera colchica* 'Dentata' or *H. helix* 'Hibernica', the walls will soon be completely masked in foliage. Maintenance is minimal if a slow-release fertilizer is used in the compost, and if an irrigation system is fitted. Such systems are available with automatic controls operated by electronic time switches, and can be installed at no great expense, supplying liquid food as well as water.

The basement areas of town houses cry out for plants, and ivies are among the few which tolerate such a gloomy situation. A low hedge of ivy at the base of the railings that divide the area from the street will prevent litter blowing in and still allow light into the windows.

Window-boxes and balconies provide the perfect situation for those ivies which look their best trailing downwards. Good examples can be seen on many hotels and office and apartment blocks

Trailing ivy enhances a terracotta pot of petunias, geraniums and standard chrysanthemum.

6

Ivy
Topiary

There is a strange paradox about topiary. The idea of clipping evergreen shrubs to produce preposterous shapes is essentially a frivolous notion, a garden joke. Yet box and yew, the traditional topiary shrubs, take a decade to achieve the desired result. A joke with a ten-year gestation period has to be a very good one to be worth waiting for.

With ivy you can have a topiary joke almost instantaneously, and I am all for as many jokes as possible in the garden. Horticulture has become rather a solemn affair, pursued with an earnest endeavour to avoid bad taste. As far as 'taste' in topiary is concerned, chessmen are considered acceptable, along with peacocks and almost any topiary figure provided it is a few centuries old. Teddy bears and Disney cartoon characters are certainly poor taste, but they are good fun.

Topiary has been in and out of fashion over the years. At the turn of this century, William Robinson, the great advocate of a natural style of gardening, was savage about it, calling it 'leprous disfigurement'. Centuries earlier the Romans thought it a civilized form of gardening and enjoyed fashioning hunt scenes, fleets of ships and all sorts of images in cypress in the first cen-

tury AD, and the Florentines during the Renaissance made apes, donkeys, oxen, bears, giants, men and women out of evergreens on frames of withies, the flexible wands of young willow trees, bent and bound into the required shapes.

In spite of William Robinson's strictures topiary remained extremely popular from the middle of the last century until the Second World War. Apart from an occasional peacock, in grand stately gardens, it was mostly seen in architectural shapes to give vertical interest to formal parterres and formally laid out rose gardens. But, like many garden plants and garden styles that have been in and out of fashion in the gardens of the gentry, the taste for topiary animals and weird and wonderful abstract shapes has been preserved in cottage gardens, and today one is more likely to come across a topiary teapot or pussycat in a small village garden than in the garden at 'the big house'.

Box and yew were the usual raw materials, but in Beeton's *All About Gardening* (1871), baskets made in ivy to decorate lawns are recommended: 'These have a pretty appearance and they may be made round or oval according to fancy. A frame of wicker-work should be made, the shape of the

PREVIOUS PAGE
A life-sized topiary elephant at Long-wood Gardens.

RIGHT *Two ivy topiary flamingos confront a pair of live peacocks at San Diego Zoo. The ivies used are 'Christian' and 'Ingrid'.*

bed about one foot or 1½ feet high, around which, on the outside, should be planted, quite thick, either the large Russian, or the small-leaved and variegated ivy. In a year or two, with a little care and attention, the wicker-work will be quite covered, when the ivy must be kept well cut in, and the earth in the basket may be raised or not at pleasure. With a little trouble, the ivy may be made to trail over wands, and form a handle to the basket.' The Russian ivy referred to is *Hedera colchica* 'Dentata', discovered in the Caucasus in the 1860s. The ivy baskets would have been filled with colourful bedding plants for the summer.

Today the light-hearted craft of topiary is very much in vogue in the USA where at one end of the scale table-top ivy topiary is an increasingly popular hobby, and at the other spectacular displays, including life-sized ivy horses and camels, can be seen at the Ladew Topiary Gardens near Baltimore, at Green Animals at Portsmouth, Rhode Island, at San Diego Zoo and at several other locations. There are also nurseries in the USA which sell topiary in pots, and frames on which to train

topiary. In the Netherlands, a long tradition of topiary production is still maintained at some of the many nurseries around Boskoop.

Ivy can be trained on frames to make geometrical topiary shapes such as pyramids, spirals and globes, or topiary sculptures of birds, animals or people. The scope is limited only by the space available and by the gardener's imagination. A topiary Noah's Ark might be the ultimate achievement to aim for, but perhaps that is a rather ambitious project for a beginner. Without skill and attention, it could end up proving the theory of a gardener I sometimes work with, who insists that all topiary animals end up looking like rabbits.

There are two methods for making topiary. One gives an instant result but is not long-lasting. It is the method used at the Ladew Gardens in the USA and by Britain's Torbay Borough Council to construct the astonishing life-size tableaux that they exhibit at Chelsea Flower Show. Themes range from the famous carousel at Longwood Gardens, Pennsylvania, to Torbay's nursery rhymes and even a full-scale London bus.

An ivy basket filled with marigolds and geraniums outside a village house at Amboise in France.

Ivy topiary swans face each other at the top of a flight of steps in a formal garden in Philadelphia, PA.

The 'instant' method of creating topiary can make use of a wide variety of plants, but ivy has two advantages over most others: firstly it is hardy in all but the harshest climates, and secondly, when used in this way it will survive for several seasons, while the topiary life-span of many other plants is just a few months.

Before explaining the Instant Method, I will describe the other method by which you can create a figure or object that will endure for decades provided you trim it regularly into shape. If the trimming regime lapses, the figure will probably turn into a rabbit, then into a giant rabbit and finally into a shapeless mess.

Since ivy is a climbing or trailing plant and not a self-supporting shrub, it needs a frame on which to train it. This can be made from stout wire, stronger metal bands or timber, depending on the size or complexity of the finished topiary figure. A variety of frames are available in the USA from specialist suppliers, listed in the Appendix. If the required shape is not readily available, sketch or photograph the desired figure and ask a metal-worker or carpenter to make it. Or, in the case of relatively simply structures, you can make them yourself.

Most books which explain how to create topiary tell you to start with a simple shape, such as a wreath, globe or spiral, then progress to more complex items. It is sound advice, but you are making topiary with ivy rather than yew or box because you are in a hurry to create a giraffe or Michelangelo's *David,* and you will want to go right ahead with it. All that is needed is courage and average do-it-yourself skill.

To explain how to construct a frame, I will take

as example a rabbit, on the principle that it is better to be the proud and confident creator of an intentional rabbit than the shamefaced creator of an accidental one. The techniques for making a topiary rabbit can be adapted for other animals, though perhaps not for Michelangelo's *David*. A sitting animal or a woman in a long skirt are relatively easy to make. It requires more skill to shape a creature with legs that will stand steadily. So the rabbit will be sitting up.

The first thing to decide is the size of the figure. It is fiddly to make anything very small unless it is a simple shape, and even the small-leaved varieties of ivy will be too coarse-textured to cover it tidily. A large figure will collapse under the weight of the ivy unless the frame is sturdy. The ideal size for a rabbit is about halfway between a life-size rabbit and a life-size man, roughly 3ft (90cm) tall.

If you can master the rabbit, ivy topiary will soon seem like child's play. Indeed, its quick results make it an ideal introduction to gardening for children. They could make ivy models of their pets, write their initials or names in ivy, and even construct an ivy Mickey Mouse or Donald Duck.

STANDARDS AND SPIRALS

For adults, particularly those with small town gardens, architectural topiary shapes are probably the most rewarding. Even for those without gardens, a pair of ivy lollipops, pyramids or cones in pots can frame the front door elegantly and will be hardier than the more usual clipped bay. A variegated ivy, such as 'Glacier' or 'Gold Dust', looks good against red brick, and one of the green, frilly

The San Diego Zoo's ivy rhinoceros immediately after planting with Hedera helix 'Schafer Three'. Automatic irrigation channels are concealed in the moss-covered frame.

WIRE RABBIT FRAME

Materials
wire cutters
pliers
fuse wire or wire ties
waterproof adhesive tape
wire, stout but pliable, about the thick-
    ness of a wire coat-hanger

Note: The ivy covering will make the
finished figure fatter than the frame, so
this should be 1in (2.5cm) smaller in
all dimensions than the required
finished figure is intended to be.

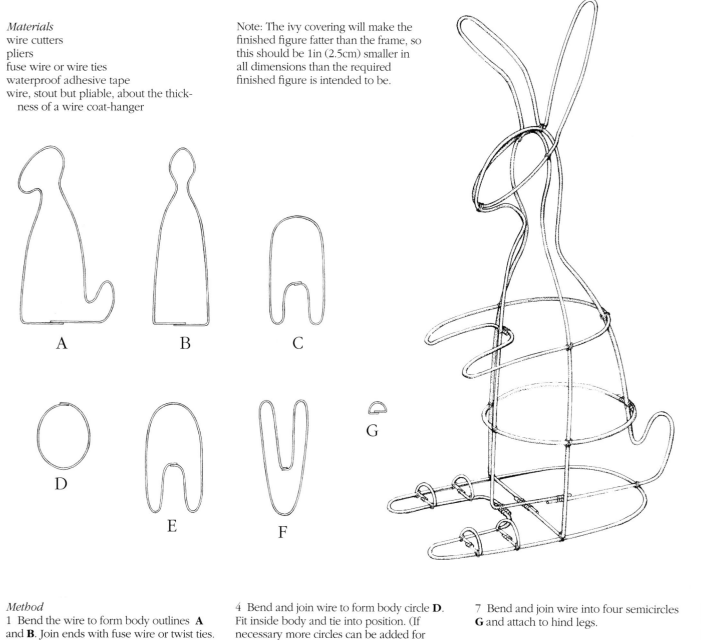

A B C D E F G

Method

1 Bend the wire to form body outlines **A**
and **B**. Join ends with fuse wire or twist ties.

2 Fit **B** inside **A** at right angles and tie at
head and base.

3 Bend and join wire to form base and hind
legs **C**. Tie to base of body.

4 Bend and join wire to form body circle **D**.
Fit inside body and tie into position. (If
necessary more circles can be added for
extra stability.)

5 Bend and join wire to form upper body and
front legs **E**. Fit inside body and tie in
position.

6 Bend and join wire to form head and
ears **F**. Fit inside head and tie in position.

7 Bend and join wire into four semicircles
G and attach to hind legs.

8 Bind all joints with waterproof tape.

9 Bend front legs and adjust ears, angle
of head and overall shape to give the rabbit
character: Brer Rabbit, Bugs Bunny, Harvey
or the White Rabbit in *Alice in Wonderland*.

forms like 'Manda's Crested' against pale stucco; the same shapes are effective as vertical accents in formal knot gardens.

With care and patience it is possible to train ivy into a standard with a spiral or plaited stem. Bay trees grown in this way are extremely expensive, because they are so slow-growing. With ivy a handsome specimen can be produced in three or four years instead of ten or more. The technique is to choose ivies with long, strong main shoots (one plant for the spiral, three for the plait), remove any side-shoots and train the main shoots loosely round a sturdy bamboo cane in the required pattern, tying them in as they grow, and rubbing out any more side-shoots that develop. When the spiral or plait has reached the required height, allow new shoots to sprout from the top, pinching out the tips from time to time to develop a bushy head. When the stem has become stout enough to be self-supporting (this will take several years),

the cane is removed from the centre. It is important to wind the stems *loosely* round the cane, or it will be impossible to remove it when the time comes.

Variations on this theme include double or treble spirals, using two or three plants instead of just one. Two spirals twisting in opposite directions works well. The stems of two ivies in the same pot can also be knotted. A series tied to demonstrate nautical knots might keep a sailor happy, and 'his and hers' ivies (a plain with a variegated or a large-leaved with a small-leaved variety) with their stems tied in a lovers' knot would make an unusual wedding present.

In a formal garden, a spiral is one of the most elegant topiary shapes, and the frame is reasonably simple to construct, provided you use new wire which is sold in a coil. Do not imagine that it can be achieved by unravelling a wire coat-hanger. The wire should be plastic covered or galva-

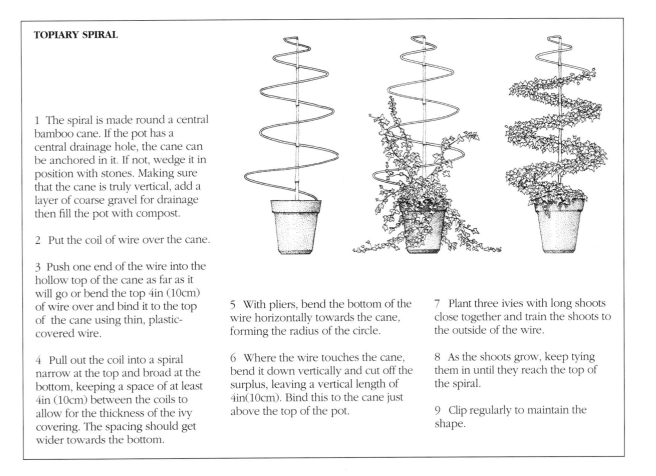

TOPIARY SPIRAL

1 The spiral is made round a central bamboo cane. If the pot has a central drainage hole, the cane can be anchored in it. If not, wedge it in position with stones. Making sure that the cane is truly vertical, add a layer of coarse gravel for drainage then fill the pot with compost.

2 Put the coil of wire over the cane.

3 Push one end of the wire into the hollow top of the cane as far as it will go or bend the top 4in (10cm) of wire over and bind it to the top of the cane using thin, plastic-covered wire.

4 Pull out the coil into a spiral narrow at the top and broad at the bottom, keeping a space of at least 4in (10cm) between the coils to allow for the thickness of the ivy covering. The spacing should get wider towards the bottom.

5 With pliers, bend the bottom of the wire horizontally towards the cane, forming the radius of the circle.

6 Where the wire touches the cane, bend it down vertically and cut off the surplus, leaving a vertical length of 4in(10cm). Bind this to the cane just above the top of the pot.

7 Plant three ivies with long shoots close together and train the shoots to the outside of the wire.

8 As the shoots grow, keep tying them in until they reach the top of the spiral.

9 Clip regularly to maintain the shape.

nized; pliable but stout enough to hold its shape. If the topiary is to be grown in a pot, make sure that the pot is the right size to be in proportion with the finished height and width of the spiral. This should be two-thirds or three-quarters as tall as the pot, and should be slightly wider at its base than the diameter of the top of the pot.

Topiary made by any of the methods described can be grown in pots so that they can be moved about the garden or brought indoors as house decoration; they can also be planted outdoors in a permanent site as part of a formal pattern or as a feature to set at the end of a vista or to come upon as a surprise round a corner. When grown in pots the plants will need annual feeding with a slow-release granular fertilizer, or more frequent liquid feeds during the growing season. Planted outdoors they will thrive for many years with little attention other than pruning.

PRE-FORMED TOPIARY

The second method, usually known as pre-formed topiary, is the Instant Method. It is used with spectacular results at Longwood Gardens in Pennsylvania, where a life-sized carousel with figures of horses, a camel, a goat and a lion were constructed using ivies to cover wire frames.

Longwood also manufactured the metal frames for the topiary animals placed at San Diego Zoo in 1991 to celebrate the Zoo's 75th birthday. Among them are an ivy giraffe, rhinoceros, gorillas and elephants.

The method is extravagant as it uses a great many plants, but the results are truly instant. The frame is completely covered with plants set into a covering of damp moss. With care a figure can be kept in good condition for two or even three seasons, and of course the frame is permanent and can be covered again with fresh plants.

Large pre-formed topiary figures, including those of Torbay and Longwood Gardens, are made in metal skeletons, with wires close enough together to hold the moss in place. The ivies are planted in each layer of moss and compost as the lining is built up from the bottom. The hollow centre is filled with styrofoam.

By using different varieties of ivy you can vary the colours and textures on a topiary figure. You can also introduce other plants for special features. The horses on the Longwood Gardens carousel started life with manes and tails of white chrysanthemums which were replaced, after the chrysanthemums had finished flowering, with long trails of white variegated ivy.

If the topiary piece is to be displayed outdoors in the garden, a hectic mixture of bright colours

---

INSTANT TOPIARY

Materials
wire cutters, pliers, scissors
stout wire
fuse wire or thin garden wire
wide-mesh chicken wire
sphagnum moss
transparent fishing line
hairpins

Method
1 Make the skeleton of the chosen shape using stout wire joined with fuse wire. Remember to make the frame thinner than the finished form will be, allowing for 1in (2.5cm) of growth on the ivy covering.

2 Mould chicken wire round the form to 'flesh out' the skeleton. Leave the top open so that you can insert the stuffing. Tall or complex figures can be made in sections and joined after stuffing and planting.

3 Line the chicken wire frame with moss, filling the centre with lightweight soil-less compost as you go. In a large piece the centre can be kept hollow by placing another layer of moss on top of the compost, then adding an inner lining of chicken wire. The layer of compost should be 2–3in (5–7.5cm) thick all round for the ivy to root into.

4 If necessary, moss can be fixed to the top of the chicken wire with fishing line.

5 At the top, close the chicken wire by twisting its cut strands together, or use fuse wire.

6 Tuck rooted ivy cuttings into the moss through the holes in the chicken wire, pushing their roots through the moss into the compost. If you want an immediate effect, place them close together so that no gaps are visible. Otherwise set them 6–9in (15–23cm) apart.

will look out of place. It is best to stick to restrained colour combinations with plenty of green. Ivy is the ideal plant to use, not only because it will quickly form a dense cover and is able to survive short periods without water, but also because of the variety of textures it can produce and the softly contrasting colours of the variegated forms.

For Sudeley Castle in Gloucestershire I designed figures of the three Tudor queens who are associated with the castle's history: Queen Catherine Parr who was King Henry VIII's widow (his sixth wife), Lady Jane Grey whose sad young life ended on the scaffold after a reign of just a few days, and Queen Elizabeth I. The three ladies wear dresses of green ivy with contrasting textures: 'Parsley Crested' for Queen Elizabeth, 'Pittsburgh' for Catherine Parr and 'Shamrock' for Lady Jane Grey. Their underskirts and ruffs are variegated 'Eva', 'Glacier' and 'Goldchild'. The green ivy overskirts are brocaded with rambler roses, white for Lady Jane Grey, dusky 'Veilchenblau' for the widowed Catherine, and 'Crimson Showers' for Queen Elizabeth, who loved rich and flamboyant clothes.

Topiary gives the gardener a chance to let the imagination have free reign, and ivy can express, in a relatively short time, whimsical flights of fancy, delusions of grandeur, or even, perhaps, a truly poetic soul. Topiary projects for my own garden include a guard dog at the door with ivy hackles up, a ghostly grey lady ('Glacier') to haunt a small spinney and an ivy dustbin to commemorate a scavenging golden Labrador.

Ivies suitable for topiary include medium and large-leaved varieties such as *H. helix* 'Caecilia', 'California', 'Ingrid', 'Ivalace', 'Kolibri', 'Königer's' and 'Star'. The smaller-leaved 'Duckfoot', 'Little Diamond', 'Miniature Needlepoint', 'Pin Oak', 'Shannon' and 'Spetchley' are also recommended. See also Ivy Chart, pp. 111–153.

A garden is not essential for ivy topiary. Indoor table-top topiary is becoming a popular hobby, and for those who lack the confidence or the nimble fingers to make their own, topiary shapes and animals can be bought at specialist garden centres and florists' shops. Suppliers of topiary frames, both planted and unplanted, are listed in the Appendix.

ABOVE LEFT *At San Diego Zoo a winter snowman is made from* Hedera helix *'Schafer Three' with an 'Ivalace' hat.*

ABOVE RIGHT *Architectural topiary: ivy pyramids in a formal garden in Philadelphia, PA.*

7

Companions
For Ivy

other plants through all four seasons and in many situations. Green or variegated ivies can be used to blend with or to set off the coloured foliage as well as the flowers of other climbers and shrubs, on walls and fences, on the ground and in containers.

On house and garden walls ivies can be used to provide a background to other climbing plants. A brick wall can be a tiresome constraint when choosing climbing plants, as many colours do not show to advantage against it. Climbing roses with colouring on the blue side of pink or the purple side of red positively swear with red brick, and the foliage of roses is too sparse to provide the flowers with a good leafy background. But their colouring is enhanced if a glossy green mantle of ivy is interposed between their flowers and the brickwork.

The dusky reds, mauves, blues and purples of clematis are also more easily appreciated against ivy than against brick, especially against the creamy mass of variegated ivies like 'Anne Marie', 'Chester' or 'Kolibri'. The yellow ivies, 'Buttercup' and 'Goldheart', complement that obliging, easy and spectacular clematis 'Jackmanii' with its rich velvety, violet flowers; this combination could be further enhanced by the red-purple leaves of *Cotinus coggygria* 'Notcutt's Variety' in front.

In most gardens wall space is at a premium, so it makes sense to double up or to treble the climbing plants and to have them weaving in and out of one another. For a striking combination of hardy climbers on a north wall, ivy can provide a fine background to the repeat-flowering buff-yellow rose 'Gloire de Dijon' and clematis 'Jackmanii', with *Tropaeolum speciosum* threading its scarlet miniature nasturtium flowers through all three of them.

In autumn the effect of ivies combined with other plants is more noticeable than earlier in the year when there is so much happening in the garden to claim the attention. Variegated ivies provide a wonderful contrast to red autumn leaves and to the red berries of pyracantha and cotoneaster. *Hedera canariensis* 'Gloire de Marengo' with the scarlet autumn leaves of Vir-

PREVIOUS PAGE
Ivy, fern and moss creep over a fallen tree, bringing a natural, woodland atmosphere to a small garden.

ABOVE *Ivy makes a dark background to the pale pink climbing rose 'New Dawn'.*

A delightful garden could be made using nothing but ivies. Their possibilities would not be exhausted even if a whole series of gardens were created, each with a completely different character, ranging from strictly architectural formality to mysterious, untamed wilderness. But only a fanatical ivy lover would dream up such a garden.

For most gardeners ivy is only one of many much-loved plants, and its chief value will lie in its cheerful luxuriance in the winter months and its ability to provide contrasts and harmonies with

ginia creeper (*Parthenocissus henryana*) rambling through it may not be a particularly original idea: I must have seen it a dozen times from the top of a London bus and from the car in market towns and quiet country villages, billowing over garden walls to enliven the street outside. But it is still a sight one could never tire of.

Other climbers with red or orange autumn leaves to plant with variegated ivies include *Vitis coignetiae,* an ornamental vine with leaves the size of dinner plates, and, among shrubs, *Berberis thunbergii, Cotinus obovatus,* many cotoneasters (with the bonus of red berries) and *Euonymus alatus.* The very fructiferous yellow-berried pyracanthas look their best against green ivies, their colouring being lost against a variegated background.

That autumn contrast of creamy variegated foliage with orange and scarlet is equally effective when the red colouring is supplied by flowers rather than leaves or berries. The fluorescent vermilion-pink rose 'Super Star', which can look garish, acquires a softer brightness when backed with a creamy mass of *Hedera canariensis* 'Gloire de Marengo'. The big dark red climbing roses 'Guinée' and 'Belle Etoile' and the scarlet 'Parkdirektor Riggers' look magnificent against a wall of variegated ivy, and the ivy in addition serves to disguise their ungainly bare legs.

Orange is a difficult colour to place in the garden, so much so that some gardeners avoid it altogether. The hard, clear brightness of pot marigolds, *Alstroemeria aurantiaca* and some berberis varieties, or the brick-orange of *Euphorbia griffithii* 'Fireglow' or *Potentilla* 'Sunset' can all be softened and cooled by a ground cover in front of them of one of the smaller-leaved cream variegated ivies such as 'Adam', 'Heise' or 'Little

Hedera colchica 'Dentata Variegata' contrasting with cotoneaster berries.

Hedera helix *'Goldheart' with* Clematis *'Ernest Markham'*.

Diamond'. The blue foliage of rue and the feathery grey leaves and cream-yellow button flowers of *Santolina neapolitana* add more soft colour to the group, and more blue can be introduced with the flowers of *Polemonium caeruleum* (Jacob's ladder), campanulas and aquilegias. The purer, softer orange flowers of *Papaver rupifragum* or *Geum* x *borisii* need less help, but are enhanced by the same ivies, with some blue and the lime yellow-green of *Euphorbia cyparissias* mixed in for bold contrast.

Colour schemes that run the risk of being overpoweringly bright can be rescued by planting either a continuous edging or interwoven groups of these tidy variegated ivies or others of sober green. Many gardeners use pastel flowers and grey foliage almost exclusively so that the garden sometimes cries out for bolder colours: scarlet,

crimson, violet, cobalt, Prussian blue, gold and sulphur. Such paint-box colours can be splashed around the garden and still form a coherent whole if ivies of restful green and cream colouring are used in the background and foreground to unite them.

When beds and borders are bright with stimulating colour, there should be an area of contrasting tranquillity. This is the place for a comfortable seat in an ivy bower. The walls and roof of the ivy-covered structure can also support other climbing plants that will supply the scented flowers that ivy cannot provide. Honeysuckle and a scented rambling rose like 'Wedding Day' or 'Paul's Himalayan Musk' can compete with the ivy or swarm up a nearby tree.

The bower will look out on to dappled shade. It may be situated in a woodland glade or, in a small

A foxglove glows against a dark, mysterious alcove framed with arborescent ivy.

garden, the shade may be cast by a single cherry tree or a gnarled orchard apple or plum. An ivy with small, delicate green leaves such as 'Scutifolia', 'Glymii' or 'Gracilis' can be allowed to climb half-way up the trunk of the nearest tree. Underneath the tree or trees the ground could be carpeted with ivies, all green-leaved but forming a tapestry of textures. Around the tree trunk the ivy sward will be relatively high, and drifts of 'Green Ripple' interlock with 'Parsley Crested'. The height of the ivies reduces gradually until at the perimeter of the shade cast by the tree, the miniature ivies 'Spetchley', 'Walthamensis' and 'Shamrock' hug the ground so that the tree appears to be growing on a low mount covered with intermeshing ivies. The same ivies form a backcloth for bulbs: snowdrops pushing up through the ground cover as soon as the winter snow melts, followed by crocus species and *Iris reticulata,* then scillas, grape hyacinths *(Muscari),* wood anemones and dwarf narcissi. In the deeper ivy cover near the base of the tree, taller narcissi, including scented jonquils 'Double Campernella' and 'Trevithian', can be followed by bluebells. Later, the untidy, dying foliage will be hidden by the ivy.

In summer, plants which are as attractive in leaf as they are in flower can grow in bold drifts among ivies. Hemerocallis have handsome pale green shoots which develop into clumps of smooth, arching, strap-shaped leaves. Their colour and vertical line will contrast well with ivies, and they will flower happily in dappled shade. A few are scented, especially the old species *Hemerocallis flava* which has been grown in gardens since the sixteenth century. Its lily-shaped flowers are clear light yellow and appear in early summer. Other hemerocallis of soft colouring include 'Bonanza', with flowers of a soft buff-yellow on shorter stems, and the pale primrose-yellow 'Kathleen Dunsford'.

Acanthus spinosus, handsome in foliage and flower, associates well with large-leaved, glossy ivies like *Hedera helix* 'Hibernica'. It is a native of Southern Europe, so Euripides would have seen it growing on the lower slopes of Mount Ida below the ivy-vested woods, and the vase-

*The grass 'Gardener's Garters' (*Phalaris arundinacea *var. Picta) with* Hedera canariensis *'Gloire de Marengo'.*

painters of his time would have noted the decorative leaves of both plants and used them in their designs. Other good foliage plants which enjoy the same woodland conditions as ivies and look natural and right growing with them in semi-wild situations include hellebores, foxgloves, *Alchemilla mollis, Brunnera macrophylla* (a wonderful weed-smotherer in shade, with big heart-shaped leaves and flowers like forget-me-nots) and bergenias.

PLANTS FOR DRY SHADE

In really difficult places where shade and poor, alkaline soil might seem to restrict the choice to ivies and nothing else, there is a surprising variety of plants which associate well with ground-cover ivies. *Iris foetidissima,* the British native Stinking or Gladwyn iris, will grow anywhere, even in pure chalk. It makes clumps of shiny dark evergreen leaves up to 2ft (60cm) tall which when crushed are said to smell of roast beef or worse. The flowers are not exciting, though the variety 'Citrina' has bigger blooms and flowers more freely than the species. 'Citrina's' flowers are soft ochreyellow with brown veining and are borne in June and July. Apart from the handsome leaves the main feature of the plant is its large seed pods in autumn, which burst open to display dense clusters of bright orange seeds which remain on the plant for several months. For foliage value alone, since it seldom flowers, *Iris foetidissima* 'Variegata' is hard to beat, with its evergreen cream-striped leaves. It is just as shade-tolerant as the species and makes a splendid winter contrast to greenleaved ivies. It would be a case of overkill to plant it with other variegated plants.

There are a few other plants which share ivy's tolerance of the dry shade which is found under greedy-rooted trees, at the base of hedges and against shady walls. In these difficult conditions it helps to add leaf-mould when planting. *Campanula latifolia* is one of the tallest, 4ft (1.2m) high, with a spread of 2ft (60cm). It has handsome leaves and the spikes of violet-blue or white bell flowers do not need staking. It flowers in July and is equally at home in the sun, but the flowers last longer in shade. It seeds itself freely which is an asset in the wild garden, though it can be a nuisance in beds and borders.

Euphorbia robbiae is a really tough ground coverer for dry shade. It spreads by means of running roots and should come with a health warning as, once it has been let into a border, it is difficult to eradicate. Its fluorescent yellow-green heads of bracts are long-lasting and, at 2ft (60cm) high, are tall enough to show well above the foliage of strong-growing ground-cover ivies. Its colouring goes well with the blue and white campanulas and, for a startling colour scheme, with the magenta flowers of honesty *(Lunaria annua)* which likes the same conditions. The ordinary honesty is a biennial, but will seed itself freely, and once you have it you are unlikely to lose it.

If the combination of magenta and lime is too violent even for a dark corner, the variegated ivies are as effective at cooling the strong colour of honesty as they are with orange flowers. The perennial honesty, *Lunaria rediviva* is more refined, with lilac-white flowers and the same translucent white, coin-shaped seed pods. Both honesties are fragrant and flower from April until June.

The native European Solomon's seal, *Polygonatum multiflorum* and the improved garden form, *P.* x *hybridum,* is a very graceful woodland plant

Hedera helix *'Deltoidea' in a tree trunk with* Tropaeolum speciosum *threading through it.*

to give height in a planting of ivies. In June its fragrant white flowers hang like lockets from arching stems about 3ft (90cm) high. After flowering the stems are sometimes completely stripped of foliage by sawfly caterpillars, but this does not seem to affect the health of the plant. There is also a form *P. falcatum* 'Variegatum', with pretty variegated leaves. Another very handsome plant, native to the USA and twice the size of the European species, is *Polygonatum commutatum* or *P. giganteum*.

In 1597 Gerard noted in his *Herball* that a preparation from the roots of Solomon's seal would take away 'any bruise gotten by falls or womens wilfulnesse, in stumbling upon their hasty husbands fists, or such like'.

Ferns and ivies associate well in the shady garden just as they do in the wild. Those that do well in dry conditions include *Dryopteris filix-mas,* the male fern. Very hardy, it remains evergreen in sheltered districts, forming an elegant sheaf of divided leaves 3ft (60cm) tall and wide. 'Crispa-cristata' is a variety of the male fern with finely toothed, wavy-edged fronds. *Polypodium vulgare* 'Cornubiense' is a beautiful Cornish form of the British polypody fern, with lacy fronds of fresh spring-green, 1ft (30cm) high. The shield ferns are evergreen and all are beautiful. Perhaps the most elegant are *Polystichum aculeatum* 'Pulcherrimum' (a form of the European hard shield fern, with silky fronds) and *Polystichum setiferum* 'Divisilobum' which has huge, beautifully poised, feathery fronds.

PLANTS FOR MOIST SHADE

In moist shade the choice of plants is greatly multiplied. There are many more ferns to choose from to give a natural effect in, for example, a streamside setting where moss-covered boulders as well as ivies will complete the cool, refreshing picture. These are the conditions to suit the most dramatic and elegant of hardy ferns, *Osmunda regalis,* the Royal Fern. Hostas, hellebores and hemerocallis are invaluable for making outstanding foliage

compositions with both green and variegated ivies, to which they each add, in their season, flowers of distinction and of subtle colouring.

Many of the plants that are happy in shade or semi-shade seem to combine attractive flowers with striking foliage. In descending order of height when in flower, I would single out the following:

Aruncus dioicus (6 x 4 ft – 1.8 x 1.2m)
The goat's beard makes a mound of light green serrated, pointed leaflets from which erect plumes of feathery cream flowers rise in June. It forms a fine backdrop to any group of ground-cover ivies, and when in flower blends in colour with those of cream variegation.

Anemone x *hybrida* (5 x 2 ft – 1.5m x 60cm)
The Japanese anemone is an absolute star in early autumn. In summer its large, dark green lobed and pointed leaves form weed-smothering clumps. The white or dusky pink flowers are held on multiple straight, smooth stems which never need staking, and unfold from grey-green globular buds that are beautiful before they open; later, the round green seed-heads are attractive. There are double forms, but the petals of the single varieties, arranged round striking, yellow stamens with a green eye, have an unrivalled purity, particularly in the classic white form 'Honorine Joubert' which has been grown in gardens since the 1850s. Sometimes slow to establish, these anemones spread generously once they get going, especially if they are in alkaline soil. They look good rising above green ivies with crimped, fingered or plain ivy-shaped leaves.

Lilium martagon (5ft x 9in – 1.5m x 23cm)
The lime-tolerant Turk's-cap lily will naturalize under tall trees and in light woodland. I have seen it growing in generous drifts in long grass at Spetchley Park in Worcestershire. It is a plant of touchingly modest grace, hanging its pretty heads of backward-curled petals. The flowers of the species are maroon-pink with darker spots and would be set off well against a background of

OPPOSITE *The glossy leaves of* Hedera algeriensis *reflect light even in the darkest corners.*

cream-variegated ivy. There is also a vigorous white form, 'Album', to grow with green ivies.

Gentiana asclepiadea (up to 3 x 2ft – 90 x 60cm)
Flowers of a pure, true blue are to be treasured anywhere in the garden. The willow gentian's flowers appear in late summer when most herbaceous plants are beginning to look tired. The flowers are held in profusion along slender arching stems with willow-like leaves and are that rare blue which is somewhere between a summer sky and the Mediterranean sea. This plant does not mind alkaline soil but must have shade or partial shade, which suits our purpose. It will grow on chalk but prefers deep, moist soil with humus added. The wonderful flower colour is accentuated when it is planted with ivies of soft cream-yellow variegation, such as 'Ingrid' or *Hedera helix hibernica* 'Sulphurea' or *Hedera colchica* 'Dentata Variegata'.

Aquilegia vulgaris (3 x 1½ ft – 90 x 45cm)
A cottage-garden plant which will stir childhood memories in many hearts, the common columbine or granny's bonnet is the easiest of plants and seeds itself freely. The distinctive and ornamental leaves are like larger versions of those of a maidenhair fern, and vary from grey to sea-green. They are attractive companions to the ivies 'Glacier' and 'Paper Doll' which, grown as ground cover, have an overall silver-grey mottled effect. The columbine's flowers are profusely borne on branching stems held well above the clump of leaves and vary in colour from purple and plum to mauve and pink. Gertrude Jekyll loved the white form and grew it with white foxgloves and white campanulas. It also associates well with honesty as it flowers at the same time.

Arum italicum (1½ x 1ft – 45 x 30cm)
This relation of the hedgerow lords-and-ladies has several assets. The greenish-white flower spathes appear in spring, followed by stout spikes of orange-red berries in summer to brighten a shady corner. The spear-shaped leaves develop in autumn and come through most winters. The

OPPOSITE *Ivies play their part in a complex harmony of texture, shape and colour.*

form 'Pictum' has dark green leaves conspicuously marbled with grey and cream; similar in colouring but very different in form to the variegated ivies, it makes a pleasing contrast.

Geranium macrorrhizum (1 x 2ft – 30 x 60cm)
Where ground cover is needed for a large, shaded area, such as a north-facing bank, and something is needed to vary and contrast with a planting of ivies, this is an unperturbable plant. It is a spreader, forming dense but tidy clumps of rounded, pale green aromatic leaves with a slight sheen. They are semi-evergreen but also turn red in autumn, so are particularly good with variegated ivies. The best flower colours are 'Album', a soft, pinkish-white, and 'Ingwersen's Variety' which is soft pink.

Other hardy geraniums are excellent to mix with ivies in a ground-cover scheme. In light shade *Geranium endressii* (1½ x 2ft – 45 x 60cm) never stops flowering all summer and goes on into autumn. *Geranium phaeum,* the Mourning Widow (2 x 1½ ft – 60 x 45cm), has nodding, darkest maroon flowers and looks mysterious growing in deep shade. A foreground of variegated ivy would cheer the widow up. There is a lovely white form, 'Album', to bring light to dark places.

Convallaria majalis (9 x 12in – 23 x 30cm)
Lilies-of-the-valley are temperamental about their site, often refusing to grow where they are planted, and at other times galloping away with unpredictable vigour. When they do this, they make weed-smothering carpets of fresh green up-standing leaves which contrast well with all kinds of ivy. The flowers retain their heavenly scent when picked. 'Fortin's Giant', a form with larger flowers, comes into flower ten days later than the species, so by planting both the flowering season can be prolonged.

Trillium grandiflorum (1½ x 1ft – 45 x 30cm)
These are choice plants to grow with the choicest, smaller-leaved ivies. The wake robin is a spring-flowering woodlander from eastern North America. It needs a position which does not dry out,

ABOVE *Dense green ivy makes a cool contrast to hot pink azaleas in a Madeira garden.*

OPPOSITE *The sober dark green ivy on the wall emphasizes the sunlit contrast of pink dahlias framed by the stone arch.*

with plenty of humus in the soil. The leaves and petals of the flowers are borne in threes, giving it a very distinctive appearance. Trilliums look their best planted in large groups of single colours. *Trillium grandiflorum* is white, and there is also a pink form 'Roseum'. *Trillium sessile* is a little shorter, and its maroon-crimson flowers are set above a striking collar of dark green leaves marbled with grey.

Erythroniums like the same moist woodland conditions and are also enhanced by the smaller, more compact ivies. They are popularly called dog's-tooth violets, but the flowers look more like miniature Turk's cap lilies. Varying in height from 6in (15cm) to 1ft (30cm), the flowers appear in spring and may be yellow, white, pink or purple. There are several named varieties available. The leaves are usually blotched with grey or brown.

The plants described are a small selection from many that will thrive in the shady conditions that ivies appreciate, chosen because they look natural and attractive planted in their company. Gardening in shade is not the problem that it is often assumed to be. There are plenty of plants to choose from, and they will produce effects that may be less showy, but are just as pleasing as the colourful displays in the sunny parts of the garden.

On a terrace, roof or balcony, pots planted permanently with ivies can have bulbs added for spring flowering, followed by annuals to last all summer: the bright, hot pinks, scarlets and magentas of geraniums and petunias contrast well with creamy-variegated ivies. With green ivies, blood-red antirrhinums look richly sombre, and for the subtle effect of green on green, pale lime-green nicotiana can be planted with green ivies.

8

IVIES
INDOORS

Today, ivies outstrip all other house plants in popularity. Their importance for indoor use has recently been emphatically endorsed by research carried out by NASA, which shows that *Hedera helix* destroys 90% of the benzene in a room. Benzene is a carcinogenic pollutant which is widespread in offices and other work places as it is found in paints, solvents and cigarette smoke. Ten plants will clean the air of a room of 1000ft sq (90m sq). So there is every reason for promoting the wider use of ivies inside buildings.

Ivy's easy-going and obliging character makes it an exceptional indoor plant. Being a woodland plant its natural preference is for cool, shady conditions that are rarely found in a city bedsit, office or hotel foyer. Yet, these are exactly the places where the millions of ivies sold every year from supermarkets and garden centres end up. It is a miracle that they do not expire within a week of arriving in the hostile environment of dry, centrally heated air, blasted by draughts every time a door is opened. They risk being killed by kindness when overzealous watering forces them to endure water-logged roots, or by neglect when left to shrivel on a sun-baked windowsill. Yet invariably they survive. They cling as tenaciously to life itself as they do to a wall or a tree trunk.

Ivies were first brought indoors in the mid-nineteenth century as part of the Victorian craze for turning the house into a jungle, and at that time books on gardening and floral decoration were full of ingenious ideas for their use. In 1872 Mary Howitt, describing her days as an art student in Munich, was charmed by the ubiquitous ivy: 'There is scarcely a room to be found which does not possess its ivy tree, and hardly a window to be seen in the street which is not rendered a bower by the festoons of ivy. It trails around the bars of the window, makes a verdant background to bouquets of flowers placed in vases or flower-pots, and often wreathes its picturesque leaves around a small statue of the Madonna.'

Other writers also noticed the delightful effects contrived with ivy in European houses, and gardening magazines were urging their readers to copy them. In Europe and the USA, questing ten-

drils of ivy invaded halls, parlours, drawing rooms and ballrooms, framing arches, doors, windows, chimneypieces, mirrors and paintings.

Ivy twined itself round newel posts and banisters and trailed from hanging baskets. Trained over a wire or timber trellis, it was planted in troughs and used as a screen for empty fireplaces in summer, and in winter as a room divider to create intimate alcoves.

Shirley Hibberd in an article in *The Floral World* in 1864 recommended training it in the form of an umbrella 'for the adornment of entrance-halls, and to intersperse among the seats and retiring places at festive gatherings . . . [it] should be grown of a suitable height and size of head to allow a couple to sit under the head for conversation; they are, in fact, a sort of lovers' retreat, and will not only contribute to the beauty of the scene . . . but often give occasions for sallies of wit and exchanges of playful badinage.' Just the thing to make a party go with a swing in those days of dowager chaperones.

Today the value of ivy for indoor decoration can extend far beyond its usefulness as a long-suffering pot plant for the windowsill or bathroom shelf. Many of the above suggestions can be adapted for modern houses and public buildings. Ivy can also be used to create original and charming living wallpaper, either by allowing the tendrils of a neat, small-leaved green variety such as 'Sagittifolia' or 'Mrs Ulin' to wander freely over a plain, light-coloured wall, or by superimposing

PREVIOUS PAGE *A modern echo of a Victorian idea.*

ABOVE *A Victorian arrangement of ivies and other foliage plants in a hanging basket.*

RIGHT *An ivy arbour for a drawing room from* Floral Decorations for the Dwelling House *by Annie Hassard (1875).*

A Victorian conservatory.

Ivy in flower arrangements.

the bolder growth of 'Manda's Crested', 'Maple Leaf' or 'Lalla Rookh' on a wallpaper with a trellis or bamboo pattern. If variegated ivies are used in this way, a dark or richly coloured wall will provide the right contrast.

Where a window or door looks on to the garden or balcony, the threshold between indoors and out can be blurred by using the same ivy to frame the window on both sides, thus bringing the garden indoors.

One of the assets of ivy is that cut branches will last for several days without water. The wild European ivy will stay the course in heated rooms for the twelve days of Christmas without wilting, and its leaves will tolerate being sprayed with gold and silver paint and glitter without shrivelling. Branches of gold and silver ivy mixed with some of plain green can form the basis for all sorts of

attractive effects. They can be tied into bunches or attached to wire frames to make garlands or miniature trees, and decorated with fir cones, nuts, ribbons and silver baubles. Holly and ivy are both traditional for Christmas decorations, and if I had to choose between them, I would rather give up the prickly holly in spite of its cheerful berries than go without ivy.

Long sprays of ivy are perfect for decorating rooms for festivals and parties at any season. They are an almost essential foliage element of flower arrangements in vases and also form the ideal basis for swags. To make a swag for draping around walls and windows or twisting round posts, nylon rope or clothes-line is suitably flexible and of the right weight to hang well. The thicker the rope, the bolder the swag. Sprays of ivy are then bound to the rope, using thin wire or

The elegance of ivy can often complement the craftsmanship of fine furniture.

A stairwell provides an opportunity to grow ivies and other climbing and trailing plants.

transparent nylon fishing line. The ivy-covered rope can be left elegantly plain and hung in graceful curves with bunches of ivy trails between each swag, or ribbons and flowers (fresh, dried or silk) or fruit and berries (real or artificial) can be added to suit a particular colour scheme, or to express a theme, whether it is exotic, avant-garde or simply very pretty.

Ivy is sentimentally associated with fidelity, and is therefore considered particularly appropriate for weddings. Many brides, including the Princess of Wales, have carried a sprig of ivy in their wedding bouquet, and when Queen Victoria's daughter, the Princess Royal, was married at the Chapel Royal, St James's Palace, garlands and pendants of ivy were used for decoration.

Hedera helix 'Deltoidea', known in America as the Sweetheart Ivy, is much used for wedding decorations and bouquets because of its dark green heart-shaped leaves. Ivy at weddings is doubly symbolic since, as well as signifying faithfulness, it is the emblem of Bacchus, the god of wine, who, as many of the guests will hope, is to play his part in the celebrations. For wedding decorations, both in church and at the reception whether it is held in a house, hotel or marquee, ivy's glossy green leaves contrast prettily with the white or pale-coloured flowers that are traditional. Long trails of ivy can be made to spiral round pillars and tent poles, to cascade from hanging baskets and to festoon the walls. Variegated ivies as well as flowers and ribbons can provide colour and also make attractive components in bridesmaids' wreaths and bouquets.

Ivies are also well suited as symbolic decorations at silver and golden wedding celebrations. For a silver wedding there is the spectacular 'White Knight', the whitest of all ivies, and for a gentler effect, the long silver-grey trails of 'Glacier'. For golden weddings, 'Goldheart', 'Buttercup' and 'Midas Touch' have the brightest colouring. Others prettily touched with gold include 'Angularis Aurea', 'Golden Ingot' and 'Gold Dust'.

For more permanent decoration of houses, hotels and offices, ivies in containers can be used

in the same ways as for balconies and roof gardens (see page 61). Mobile wooden troughs and Versailles tubs, mounted on castors, are particularly useful for hotels, conference centres, art galleries and anywhere where adaptability is important. They can be moved easily from one room to another, or from indoors on to terraces.

Moss sticks are useful for training ivy as a vertical feature. They consist of bamboo canes or lengths of rigid plastic pipe bound with a layer of sphagnum moss held in place with string or plastic micromesh. The diameter of most moss sticks is 1½ in (4cm), and they are sold by florists in various lengths up to 6ft (1.8m). If one stick is planted in a pot, two or three ivy plants trained spirally

Ivy plays its part in a winter arrangement of fir cones, fungi and evergreen foliage.

Lady in the Kitchen *by Viggo Johansen (1851–1935).*

around it will make a dense, slender pillar which can be kept trim by clipping over it now and then. Several ivy-covered moss sticks of different heights used in one pot or container create a sculptural effect. The same effects can be achieved at less expense by using plain bamboo canes, but moss sticks have the advantage of retaining moisture which helps the ivies to stay healthy.

Robust climbing ivies are best for this purpose. It is a good opportunity to use ivies that are dam-

aged by severe frosts when grown outdoors, like *Hedera algeriensis* which is fast-growing with very large glossy green leaves, and the grey-and-white variegated *canariensis* clone, the much-loved 'Gloire de Marengo'. Others which are perfectly frost resistant but will also do well grown in this way include *H. helix* 'Green Feather', 'Glacier', 'Green Ripple' and 'Parsley Crested'.

Where there is enough space for a really large container and a tall supporting frame, one or two ivies can be trained to such a height that they achieve the proportions of a small tree. This looks especially dramatic when used to decorate a stair-well, or in other positions where it can be seen from above as well as from below.

When indoor ivies outgrow their pots or threaten to strangle their owner with rampant growth, or if they show serious signs of stress, they can be moved out into the garden and planted in the open ground. This is best done in late spring when the climate outdoors is not too different from that of the room they are moved from. The shock to the system will be reduced and they will have all summer to settle into their new environment.

Professional and amateur flower arrangers are well aware of the excellent qualities of ivy as a graceful trailer and a provider of background greenery. Constance Spry, the doyenne of her art, was very taken with ivies that she saw on a visit to the USA in 1947 and brought home cuttings which she persuaded the nurseryman Thomas Rochford to propagate from. This was something of a landmark in the ivy industry which has gone from strength to strength ever since.

Constance Spry's Victorian forerunners were interested in using individual ivy leaves in their decorations, as well as sprays and branches. Illustrations in *Flower and Fruit Decoration* by T. C. Marsh (1862) show ivy leaves arranged neatly as borders to bowls of flowers and fruit. She recommended a border of ivy for a dish of nectarines and peaches and tree ivy with its black berries to decorate a bowl of oranges. Ivy also often trailed from the elaborate, tiered centrepieces placed on the genteel dinner tables of that period and was even used to create vases such as an ivy-twined tripod shown in a florist's catalogue of 1900. In the centre a bird's nest was poised to hold the flower arrangement.

By way of contrast, simplicity was the keynote a century later when Margery Fish wrote: 'There was no green leaf of any kind to pick except ivies, and I filled the low bowls which suit my heavy oak tables with sprigs of ivy – trails of the frilled "Parsley" ivy, *Hedera helix cristata* [today the correct name is *H. helix* 'Parsley Crested'], with its warm tones in winter, and snippets of small variegated ivies.' A simple winter arrangement of this kind affords the pleasure of studying in detail the individual leaves and the elegant way they are held on the stem. Those varieties which change colour in cold weather, developing bronze or red overtones, are particularly fascinating, and there are others on which the veins become whiter and more prominent in winter. When there are no fresh flowers available, branches or sprigs of ivy will breathe life into arrangements of dried and silk flowers bringing a bright freshness to the whole ensemble.

At any time of year ivy foliage provides contrasts of form and colour in flower arrangements of different styles. In large set pieces for grand occasions, long sprays of large-leaved green ivies or others with unusual leaves such as 'Asterisk', 'Manda's Crested' or 'Triton' can be used to form the framework of the arrangement, trailing sideways and downwards from a container set on a pillar. For small table arrangements even a few flowers can have an impact if they are backed with plain and variegated ivies with delicate small leaves, such as 'Adam', 'Eva', 'Merion Beauty', 'Pin Oak' or 'Miniature Needlepoint'.

In everyday flower arrangements at home, a few sprigs of native ivy surrounding a simple bunch of primroses is charming in spring; long trails bring an elegant line to an urn of berries and seed-heads in autumn, and in high summer creamy variegated ivies complement the voluptuous crimsons of peonies or roses.

Ivy will outlast most other cut foliage and may even help flowers to last longer in water: Virginia

Woolf gives a tip in *Jacob's Room,* describing a discussion on how to keep flowers fresh throughout a party, though she treats the idea sceptically herself: 'On the whole, though the price is sinful, carnations pay best: – it's a question, however, whether it's wise to have them wired. Some shops advise it. Certainly it's the only way to keep them at a dance; but whether it's necessary at dinner parties, unless the rooms are very hot, remains in dispute. Old Mrs Temple used to recommend an ivy leaf – just one – dropped into the bowl. She said it kept the water pure for days and days. But there is some reason to think that old Mrs Temple was mistaken.'

I think so, too. But even if it does not have the power to prolong the life of other cut flowers, ivy itself will last in water for two weeks or more, which makes it one of the most obliging plants for flower arrangements, as well as the best and most trouble-free of house plants.

Because of their susceptibility to winter damage, certain ivy varieties do better as house plants than in the open garden, notably the following: *H. helix* 'Alt Heidelberg', 'Big Deal', 'Bruder Ingobert', 'California', 'Cockle Shell', 'Hazel', 'Kolibri', 'Rusche', 'Sinclair Silver Leaf', 'Spectre', 'Trinity' and 'Zebra'.

Looking towards the conservatory from the Chinese Room at Middleton Park, Oxfordshire (1840).

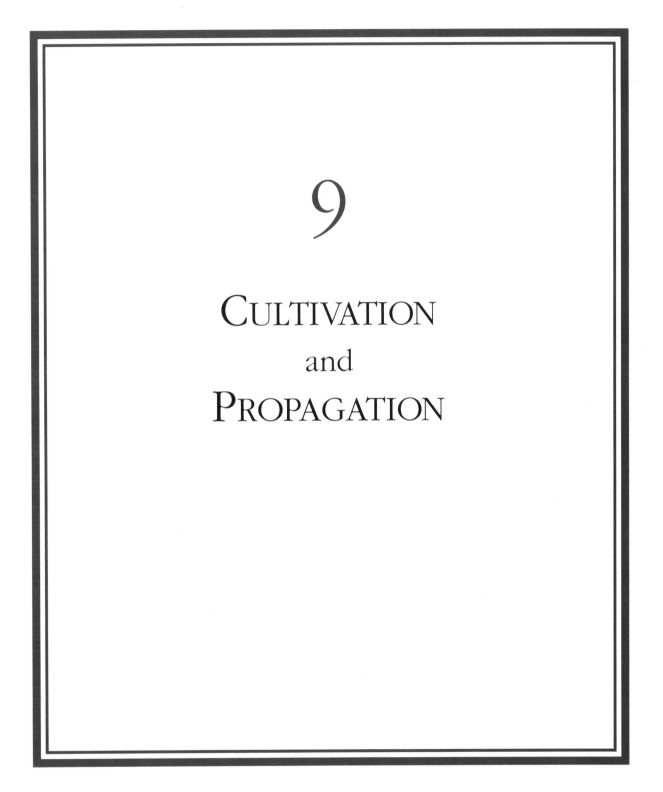

9

CULTIVATION
and
PROPAGATION

PREVIOUS PAGE
*Different varieties
of ivy can
transform the
surroundings.*

ABOVE *A vigorous
variegated ivy
climbing on a
Georgian London
house.*

I have made much in earlier chapters of the fact that most ivies are tolerant of poor conditions. However, like all plants, they will respond gratefully if their preferences are catered for at the planting stage and during their establishment. It used to be thought that *Hedera helix,* the parent of the majority of ornamental ivies, prefers an alkaline soil but there is no proof that this is so, and the plant certainly does not insist on it. At the base of old walls there is often some mortar rubble and that suits ivy very well. On very acid soil the pH can be adjusted by digging in lime in the form of old mortar or crushed chalk before planting. *Hedera canariensis* and *Hedera colchica* are happiest in neutral to acid soil. Being deep-rooted, ivies establish best in a deep and wide, well-dug hole.

All ivies will grow in sun or shade, but full sun, for example on a south-facing wall, will scorch the leaves of many of the variegated ivies. All ivies grow more slowly in sun than in shade and the leaves tend to be smaller. At the same time, ivies

with yellow variegation need good light if they are to colour well – in deep shade the yellow colouring will fade to lime-green. Although most ivies are frost-hardy, some, such as varieties of the Canary Island ivy *(Helix canariensis),* may suffer damage to the leaves, or leaf loss, if exposed to desiccating winter winds or to strong winter sunshine. A position sheltered from both wind and sun should be found for these.

Once established, ivies never seem to need watering or feeding, but in their first season after planting, the ground around the roots should not be allowed to dry out. The structure of very free-draining soils can be improved by digging in bulky organic manure and on poorly drained sites coarse grit should also be added. A 2in (5cm) deep mulch of spent mushroom compost or pulverized forest bark will help to conserve soil moisture and eliminate competition from weeds while the ivies become established.

Although there is no stopping them once started, ivies tend to hang back shyly when first planted. There is an old saying about ivy: 'the first year it sleeps, the second year it creeps, the third year it leaps'. If truly cosseted any ivy may leap in the first year, but do not be surprised if it is diffident to start with. Ivies planted in ordinary good garden soil do not need fertilizer although a few doses of liquid manure during the growing season will hurry them on in the first few years.

WALL AND FENCE COVERING

An 1860 issue of *The Cottage Gardener and Country Gentleman* gives the following counsel of perfection, which is as good advice today as it was then:

> The first thing to do covering an unsightly wall
> with ivy quickly is a thorough good rich deep
> dug border well drained. The better the border
> the faster the ivy will cover it. Any wall under
> ten feet high may be covered in one season
> and a half by planting ivy from seven to ten
> feet high out of pots about two feet apart. We
> have done so nearly four years back and by
> the middle of the second season every brick
> was covered; but for a higher wall we would
> use stronger dwarf plants and put them out in
> about April at one foot apart and water them
> with liquid manure in summer for the first two
> or three years. No plant we know will pay better
> for heavy watering and with the garden
> engine to dash water among the leaves. When
> once the wall is covered the labour and care
> begins. The knife, the eye, the hand and the
> brain must go in harmony to 'keep' the ivy as
> short as the lawn. No shoot is allowed to get
> one inch from the wall; and like seedlings the
> shoots must be thinned where too close and so
> must the leaves. Also the very long and the very
> short stalked ones, but there is not one of a
> thousand takes such pride in ivy as to make a
> model of it.

The garden engine referred to was a watering contraption in common use before the days of

garden taps and hosepipes. The water was contained in a tank mounted on wheels, which could be moved around the garden. The pruning advice seems more appropriate to the country gentleman than the cottage gardener; he probably employed servants to do the time-consuming, meticulous work recommended. The ordinary or cottage gardener of today can be content with clipping ivy over with garden shears once or twice a year to keep the growth dense and fresh.

It is important to keep ivy cut back at the top of

Ivy as architecture.

ABOVE Hedera helix 'Green Ripple'.

OPPOSITE Hedera helix 'Goldheart' with the dusky Vitis Vinifera 'Purpurea'.

a wall or fence to prevent it from developing the adult form which can look untidy and may, by its top-heavy weight, pull the whole plant away from the wall and, if this is unsound, pull down parts of the wall with it. On house walls, ivy should never be allowed to reach the guttering or the roof tiles as it may creep under them and dislodge them as the stems thicken.

On trees too, it is advisable to prevent ivy from growing high enough to reach its arborescent phase or the weight may pull the tree down in high winds. However, as the adult ivy phase is the most attractive to wildlife it is a good idea to allow it to develop where it can do no harm, such as on a low solid wall or in a hedge.

Planting distances of 2ft (60cm) for large plants and 1ft (30cm) for smaller plants will ensure rapid and total coverage of a wall. However, the same results can be obtained by planting at 3ft (90cm) distances – it will just take a little longer. If the aim

10

THE IVY CHART

Botanists disagree about the number of distinct species in the *Hedera* genus. In the chart that follows only species generally recognized as distinct are included, shown in alphabetical order and capital letters; known cultivars, varieties and clones are listed beneath the species from which they are derived.

The naming of ivies is still in a state of confusion. Although an official International Register of Ivies now exists, under the auspices of the American Ivy Society, different nurseries may list identical ivies under different names, and there is often a discrepancy between names used in Europe and names of the same variety used in the USA. Synonyms and 'look-alikes' have therefore been included and cross-referenced in the chart.

HARDINESS

Ivies are much hardier than is generally supposed. A few may be cut to the ground by hard frosts but they generally shoot again from the base the following spring. Some may suffer leaf damage in severe winters, but this can be minimized by planting doubtful varieties in sheltered sites, out of drying winds and direct sun, and by covering the root area with straw, bracken or conifer branches before the onset of winter. It is a sound precaution to root a few cuttings for growing indoors.

For horticultural purposes, the vast American mainland has been divided into a number of zones with average winter night temperatures.

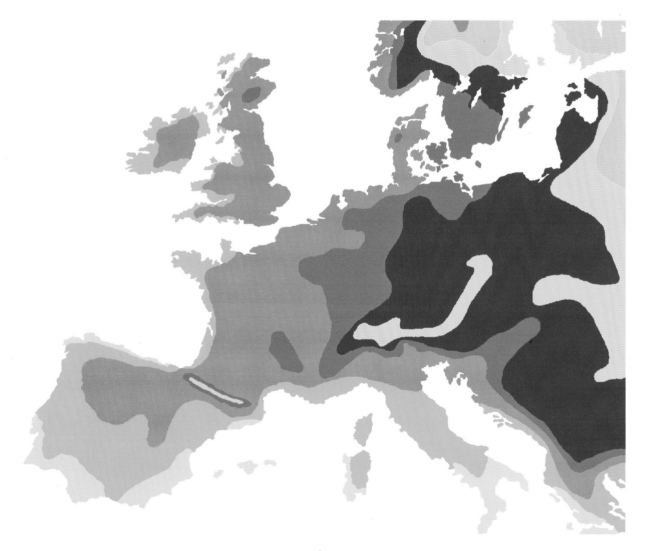

*Zone Map:
Northern Europe*

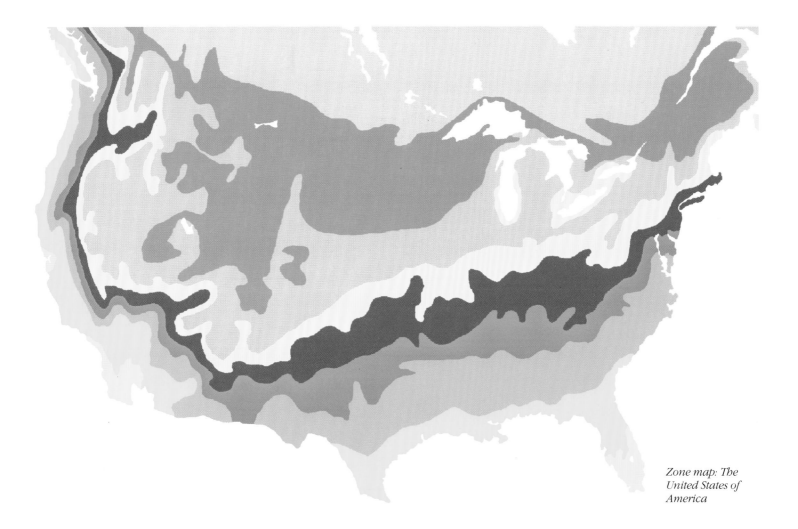

Zone map: The United States of America

Plants in Zone 5, for example, will survive at -20 to -10˚F (-29 to -23˚C), those in Zone 6 at -10 to 0˚F (-23 to -18˚C), in Zone 7, 0 to 10˚F (-18 to -12˚C) and in Zone 8 temperatures of 10 to 20˚F (-12 to -7˚C). The climate zones are intended as a general guide. Local micro-climates vary considerably and conditions in a particular garden can be harsher or milder than indicated in the relevant zone. All ivies are hardy in Britain and much of Northern Europe (Zone 8 and probably Zone 7). The findings of hardiness trials carried out by the American Ivy Society at various sites in the USA may show that some varieties are hardier than was previously assumed.

KEY TO ZONE MAPS

☐	Zone 1	-50˚ (not shown)	■ Zone 6	-10˚ to 0˚
☐	Zone 2	-50˚ to -35˚	▨ Zone 7	0˚ to 10˚
▨	Zone 3	-35˚ to -20˚	▨ Zone 8	10˚ to 20˚
▨	Zone 4	-20˚ to -10˚	☐ Zone 9	20˚ to 30˚
☐	Zone 5	-20˚ to -10˚	☐ Zone 10	30˚ to 40˚

Plant name	Description	Zone	Leaf shape	Leaf Size	Rate of growth
HEDERA ALGERIENSIS	See *Hedera canariensis*. Native to Algeria.				
HEDERA AZORICA	Vigorous. Light green leaves with 5, sometimes 7 blunt lobes.	6	Fan shaped	Large	Fast
Pico	Broad leaves, with unbroken margins and heavily netted.	7	Heart shaped		
Variegata	Similar to *H. azorica*, but strongly variegated.	7	Fan shaped	Large	Slow
HEDERA CANARIENSIS Similar varieties: *H. algeriensis*; *H.algeriensis* 'Montgomery', 'Monty', 'Ravensholst'	Found in the Canary Islands and named in 1808 by the German botanist Karl Willdenow. Vigorous with glossy dark green leaves, shiny wine-red stems and leaf stalks. In commerce today as *H. algeriensis* or *H. canariensis* 'Algerian'. Drought resistant.	6	Heart shaped	Large	Fast
Gloire de Marengo Synonym: *H. canariensis* 'Variegata'	Similar to the species, but less hardy and light green leaves heavily variegated, most pronounced on young leaves. The fastest of variegated ivies.	7	Heart shaped	Large	Fast
Gold Leaf	See *H. canariensis* 'Striata'; *H. colchica* 'Sulphur Heart'.				
Margino Maculata	Liable to winter damage, but recovers. Good trained as pyramid indoors. Glossy leaves, red-stalked.	7	Heart shaped	Large	
Striata Synonyms: 'Gold Leaf', 'Yellow Bird'	Robust, unlobed leaves of lustrous dark green, the centre sometimes faintly splashed with yellow.	6	Heart shaped	Large	Fast
Variegata	See 'Gloire de Marengo'.				
Yellow Bird	See 'Striata'.				
HEDERA COLCHICA Synonym: 'My Heart'	The Persian ivy, native to the Caucasus, Balkans and Turkey. Dark green leathery leaves with a waxy quilted surface; spicy scent when crushed.	5	Heart shaped	Large	
Batumi	Collected by Roy Lancaster in 1979 in Georgia, USSR. Aromatic leaves, 3-lobed, with shiny quilted and dark green upper surfaces, maroon in winter. Maroon leaf stalks.	8	Heart shaped	Large	Fast
Dentata	Vigorous and needs space. Known as elephant's ears from its leathery leaves as much as 8 x 7in (20 x 17cm), rich mid green and hanging downwards on long purplish stalks. Very hardy.	5	Heart shaped	Large	
Dentata Variegata	As 'Dentata' but light green leaves dramatically splashed with grey-green; uneven creamy-yellow margins occasionally cover half or entire leaf. Needs space.	5	Heart shaped	Large	Fast
Gold Leaf	See *H. canariensis* 'Striata'; *H. colchica* 'Sulphur Heart'.				

Key:

Symbols in green indicate better than average performance

| Ivy leaf | Heart shaped | Fan shaped | Diamond shaped | Curly/ crested | Bird's-foot | Small | Medium | Large | Fast | Slow |

Variegation	Winter Colour	Uses		
		Climber	Ground cover	Outdoor pots
			Ground cover	Outdoor pots
Cream-yellow		Climber	Ground cover	Outdoor pots
	✓	Climber	Ground cover	Outdoor pots
White-grey		Climber	Ground cover	Indoor pots / Outdoor pots
Lemon-cream mottled		Climber		Indoor pots
Yellow		Climber	Ground cover	
		Climber	Ground cover 2ft/60cm apart	Outdoor pots
	✓	Climber	Ground cover	
		Climber	Ground cover 3ft/90cm apart	
Cream-yellow		Climber	Ground cover 3ft/90cm apart	Outdoor pots

Legend:

| + Grafts | Climber | Trailer | Hanging baskets | Ground cover | Indoor pots | Outdoor pots | Topiary | Bonsai |

Hedera canariensis 'Gloire de Marengo'

Hedera colchica 'Dentata Variegata'

Plant name	Description	Zone	Leaf shape	Leaf size	Rate of growth
My Heart	See *H. colchica*.				
Paddy's Pride	See 'Sulphur Heart'.				
Sulphur Heart Synonyms: 'Gold Leaf', 'Paddy's Pride'	Leaves similar to 'Dentata' with irregular central variegations.	5	🍂	◼	🐇
HEDERA HELIX	The English ivy but found throughout Europe, from southern Scandanavia in the north to western USSR in the east. The ancestor of most ornamental ivies. Good in poor conditions.	5	🍃	◼	🐇
Aalsmeer	Similar to 'Domino'.				
Abundance	Similar to 'Cascade'.				
Adam Similar variety: 'Ardingly'	Outstanding ivy, tidy and bushy but spreading with graceful trails. Light grey-green leaves with variegated margins, pink in winter.	7	🍃	▫	
Ahorn	Broad green leaves with sharply pointed lobes.	8	🍁	◼	
Albany Synonyms:'Bunch','Dankeri'	Broad green ivy-shaped leaves on oddly flattened stems.	8	🍃	◼	🐢
Alpha	Similar to 'Fan'.				
Alten Brucken	Elegant, 3-pointed leaves with long central lobe; yellow-speckled in spring, all green by late summer.	8	🍃	▫	
Alt Heidelberg	Compact short-jointed miniature from Neuberg Monastery near Heidelberg. Dark green oak-like leaves held tight against stem. Old plants produce long, untypical shoots which should be pruned out. Ideal in rock gardens.	8	🍃	▫	🐢
Ambrosia	Good pot plant with pink stems; round convoluted leaves.	8	🍁	▫	
Anchor Similar varieties: 'Long Point', 'Tribairn'	Green leaves with 5 slender points; graceful trails.		✚	◼	
Angularis Aurea Similar variety: 'Spectabilis Aurea'.	Yellow spring leaves, mottled green in summer and chocolate brown in winter. Needs sun. Colour develops as plants mature.	8	🍃	◼	🐇
Anne Borche	Similar to 'Anne Marie'.				
Anne Marie Similar varieties: 'Anne Borche', 'Hahnii', 'Harald'	Popular indoor pot plant, branching and throwing out long trails. It is also an all-purpose garden ivy. The grey-green leaves are strongly variegated.	8	🍃	◼	

Key:

Symbols in green indicate better than average performance

🍃	🍂	🍁	🍃	🍁	✚	▫	◼	◼	🐇	🐢
Ivy leaf	Heart shaped	Fan shaped	Diamond shaped	Curly/ crested	Bird's-foot	Small	Medium	Large	Fast	Slow

Variegation	Winter Colour	Uses						
Yellow		Climber		Ground cover (3ft/90cm apart)		Outdoor pots		
		Climber		Ground cover				
White-cream	✓	Climber	Trailer	Ground cover	Indoor pots	Outdoor pots		
		Climber	Trailer	Hanging baskets Ground cover	Indoor pots	Outdoor pots		
				Ground cover	Indoor pots	Outdoor pots		Bonsai
Yellow		Climber		Ground cover				
					Indoor pots			Bonsai
Cream					Indoor pots	Outdoor pots		
		Climber	Trailer	Hanging baskets Ground cover	Indoor pots	Outdoor pots		
Yellow	✓	Climber						
Cream		Grafts Climber	Trailer	Hanging baskets Ground cover	Indoor pots	Outdoor pots	Topiary	

'Paddy's Pride'

'Adam'

Key:

Grafts	Climber	Trailer	Hanging baskets	Ground cover	Indoor pots	Outdoor pots	Topiary	Bonsai

Plant name	Description	Zone	Leaf shape	Leaf size	Rate of growth
Appaloosa	Variegated ivy similar to 'Manda's Crested'.	7	🍁	◼	
Arapahoe	Five-lobed leaves, the central lobe prominent and pointed.	8	🍁	◼	
Ardingly	Similar to 'Adam'.				
Arrowhead	Similar to 'Little Gem'.				
Asterisk	Outstanding ivy with leaves consisting of 5–7 long narrow points like a star.	7	✳	◼	
Astin	Seven-lobed green leaves, curled at margins.	8	🍁	⬛	
Atropurpurea Synonym: 'Purpurea' Similar varieties: 'Glymii', 'Nigra', 'Woerneri'	Elegant and grown for its black-purple winter colour, best on exposed cold walls. Arrow-shaped young leaves mature to typical ivy shape.	7	🍃	◼	🐇
Baden-Baden	Green-leaved ivy, leaves like starfish with 5 deeply slender points of near equal length.	8	🍁	◼	
Baltica Similar varieties: 'Bulgaria', 'Rumania', 'Yalta'	Ultra-hardy, small-leaved ivy, whitish veins.	3	🍃	◦	
Big Deal Similar varieties: 'Knulch', 'Kurios'	Known as the geranium ivy and barely recognizable as an ivy, with rounded puckered leaves on short zig-zag trails.	8	🍁	⬛	
Bill Archer	See 'Excalibur'.				
Blodwen	Creamy margins to sharp-pointed leaves of ivy shape.	8		◦	
Bodil	Similar to 'Domino'.				
Boskoop	Bred in Holland. Leathery, wedge-shaped dark green leaves are set close to the stems, frilled and pointing down. Outstanding.	8	🍁	◼	
Brightstone	Five-pointed leaves with broad variegation at margins.	8	🍃	⬛	
Brokamp Synonyms: 'Imp', 'Longifolia', 'Salicifolia' Similar varieties: 'Gavotte', 'Sylvanian'	Distinctive German ivy, dense and with long trails. The long, dark green and glossy leaves are held close to stems. They turn bronze in winter in poor soils. Drought-resistant.	7	🍂	◼	🐇

Key:

Symbols in green indicate better than average performance

🍃	🍂	🍁	🍃	🍁	✳	◦	◼	⬛	🐇	🐢
Ivy leaf	Heart shaped	Fan shaped	Diamond shaped	Curly/ crested	Bird's-foot	Small	Medium	Large	Fast	Slow

Variegation	Winter Colour	Uses								
White		Climber	Trailer	Hanging baskets	Ground cover	Indoor pots	Outdoor pots		Topiary	
		Climber	Trailer		Ground cover	Indoor pots	Outdoor pots			
		Climber			Ground cover	Indoor pots	Outdoor pots		Topiary	
		Climber	Trailer	Hanging baskets	Ground cover	Indoor pots	Outdoor pots			
	✓	Climber			Ground cover					
		Climber	Trailer	Hanging baskets		Indoor pots	Outdoor pots			
		Climber			Ground cover					
		Climber	Trailer	Hanging baskets		Indoor pots	Outdoor pots			Bonsai
Cream		Trailer	Hanging baskets			Indoor pots				
		Climber	Trailer	Hanging baskets		Indoor pots	Outdoor pots		Topiary	
White/ cream-white		Climber	Trailer	Hanging baskets	Ground cover	Indoor pots	Outdoor pots			
	✓	Climber	Trailer	Hanging baskets	Ground cover	Indoor pots	Outdoor pots		Topiary	

'Brokamp'

'Boskoop'

| + | Grafts | | Climber | | Trailer | | Hanging baskets | | Ground cover | | Indoor pots | | Outdoor pots | | Topiary | | Bonsai |

119

Plant name	Description	Zone	Leaf shape	Leaf size	Rate of growth
Bruder Ingobert Synonym: 'Ingobert'	A sport of 'Glacier' named after Brother Ingobert at Neuberg Monastery. Grey-green variegated leaves on purple-red stems.	7	Ivy leaf	Medium	
Bulgaria	Similar to 'Baltica'.				
Bunch	See 'Albany'.				
Buttercup Similar variety: 'Light Fingers'	Outstanding, all-yellow ivy with 5-pointed leaves which in shade, indoors and on the ground turn dull lime-green. Good against brick walls, behind red-berried shrubs and with all green ivies.	7	Ivy leaf	Medium	Fast
Caecilia Synonym: 'Clotted Cream'	The 3-lobed leaves are cream mottled with green, and have crimped margins.	8	Fan shaped	Medium	
Caenwoodiana	See 'Pedata'.				
Caenwoodiana Aurea	In spite of the name, a green-leaved ivy, only fleetingly suffused with yellow in spring, otherwise similar to 'Pedata'.	7	Bird's-foot	Medium	Fast
Calico	Similar to 'Kolibri', but more silvery.				
California Similar variety: 'Holly'	Dense and bushy, with plenty of trails; mid- to dark-green leaves.	6	Fan shaped		Fast
California Fan	See 'Fan'.				
California Gold	Compact and bushy ivy with rounded, light green speckled leaves.	8	Heart shaped	Medium	
Caramellow	An introduction from Holland, with jade-green, white-streaked leaves.		Ivy leaf	Small	
Carolina Crinkle	Bushy, with 7 or more sharply pointed curving lobes; light green with prominent veins.	7	Fan shaped	Small	
Cascade Similar variety: 'Abundance'	Plenty of branching trails set with mid green, light-veined leaves.	7	Ivy leaf	Small	Fast
Cathedral Wall	Similar to 'Trustee'.				
Cavendishii Synonym: 'Marginata'	Probably named in 19th C. after the Duke of Devonshire. Tri-angular grey-streaked leaves. The arborescent form is outstanding.	8	Ivy leaf	Small	Slow
Ceridwen Synonym: 'Golden Ester'	The Welsh name means fair and graceful; 3-pointed yellow leaves are brushed with 2 shades of soft green. A bushy plant with plentiful trails.	7	Ivy leaf	Medium	
Chester	One of the best variegated ivies for general use. Good climber, trailer and pot plant. Triangular leaves start lime-green with dark centres, the margins maturing to lemony-cream.	7	Ivy leaf	Medium	
Chicago	Similar to 'Pittsburgh'.				

Key:

Symbols in green indicate better than average performance

Ivy leaf	Heart shaped	Fan shaped	Diamond shaped	Curly/ crested	Bird's-foot	Small	Medium	Large	Fast	Slow

Variegation	Winter Colour	Grafts	Climber	Trailer	Hanging baskets	Ground cover	Indoor pots	Outdoor pots	Topiary	Bonsai
Grey		○	●	●	●		●	●	○	
Yellow			○							
Cream			●	●	●		●	●	●	
Yellow			●							
		○				○	○	○	○	○
Yellow/ cream-yellow		○		●	●		○	○	○	
White		○		●	●		○	○		
		○	●	●	●	●	●	●		
			●	●	○	●	●	●	●	
White-grey			●					●		
Yellow			●	●	○		○	○	●	
Cream-yellow			●	●			●	●		

Grafts · Climber · Trailer · Hanging baskets · Ground cover · Indoor pots · Outdoor pots · Topiary · Bonsai

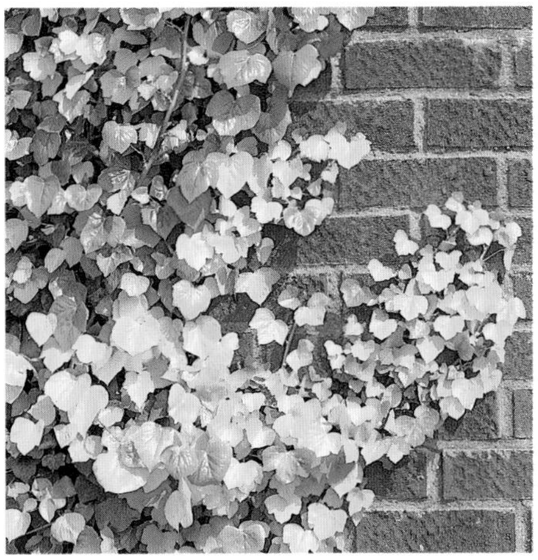

'Buttercup'

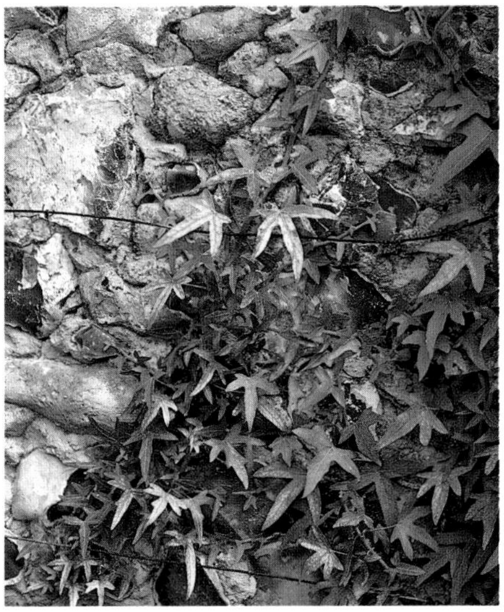

'Caenwoodiana aurea'

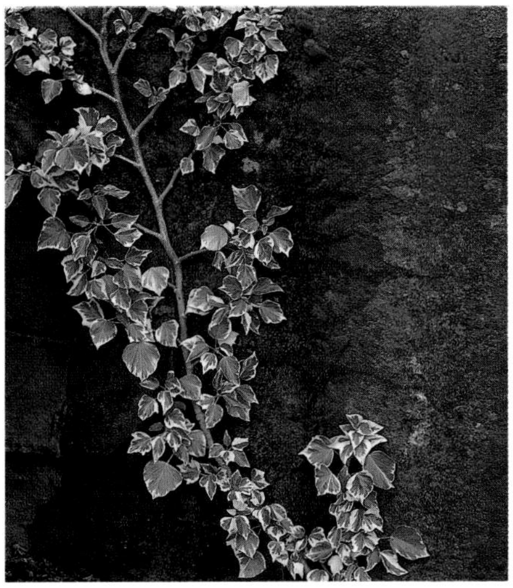

'Cavendishii'

Plant name	Description	Zone	Leaf shape	Leaf size	Rate of growth
Chicago Variegata	See 'Ingrid'.				
Choice	Similar to 'Goldchild', but larger.				
Christian	Similar to 'Direktor Badke'.				
Clotted Cream	See 'Caecilia'.				
Cockle Shell	Outstanding ivy of branching and trailing growth. Rounded light green leaves with upturned margins and prominent veins.	7	(fan shaped)	(small)	(slow)
Congesta	Dwarf shrubby ivy with stiffly erect stems closely set with dark green, light-veined leaves. Excellent for rock gardens and bottles.	7	(ivy leaf)	(small)	(slow)
Conglomerata	Dwarf creeping ivy with rounded dark green leathery leaves of ivy or fan shape. Ideal as contrast to 'Congesta' in rock gardens and on drystone walls. Bottle gardens.	7		(small)	(slow)
Crispa	Similar to 'Parsley Crested'.				
Cristata (Crestata)	See 'Parsley Crested'.				
Curley Q	See 'Dragon Claw'.				
Curly Locks	See 'Manda's Crested'.				
Curvaceous	Trailing ivy with 3- to 5-lobed leaves, light green with grey-green centres and wide variegated margins.	8	(fan shaped)	(medium)	
Cuspidata Minor	Glossy green, white-veined leaves make attractive herringbone tracery on walls.	7	(heart shaped)	(medium)	
Cyrano de Bergerac	Named from the long and blunt central lobe of the variably shaped leaves, said to resemble a nose.	7		(medium)	
Dankeri	See 'Albany'.				
Dealbata	Similar to 'Minor Marmorata', but with smaller leaves, splashed and spotted. Some nurseries describe the variegations as gold rather than white. Colours best in poor soils.	7	(ivy leaf)	(small)	(fast)
Dean	See 'Heise'.				
Deltoidea Synonyms:'Hastata', 'Ovata', 'Sweetheart' Similar variety: 'Sark'	Popularly known as sweetheart ivy from the shape of the dark green leaves. Stout stems and purple-bronze winter colour.	7	(heart shaped)	(medium)	(slow)
Denmark	Bushy trailing miniature ivy.		(fan shaped)	(small)	(slow)

Key:

Symbols in green indicate better than average performance

Ivy leaf	Heart shaped	Fan shaped	Diamond shaped	Curly/ crested	Bird's-foot	Small	Medium	Large	Fast	Slow

Variegation	Winter Colour	Uses
		Grafts · Trailer · Hanging baskets · Ground cover · Indoor pots · Outdoor pots
		Outdoor pots · Bonsai
		Ground cover · Indoor pots · Outdoor pots · Bonsai
White		Climber · Trailer · Hanging baskets · Indoor pots · Outdoor pots
		Climber
		Trailer · Ground cover · Outdoor pots
Cream-white		Climber · Indoor pots · Outdoor pots
		Climber · Ground cover · Indoor pots · Outdoor pots
White		Climber · Trailer · Hanging baskets · Ground cover · Indoor pots · Outdoor pots

'Comglomerata'

'Manda's Crested'

Grafts · Climber · Trailer · Hanging baskets · Ground cover · Indoor pots · Outdoor pots · Topiary · Bonsai

Plant name	Description	Zone	Leaf shape	Leaf size	Rate of growth
Diana	Glossy green leaves with raised veins; the broad lobes terminate in long curved points.	8	Ivy leaf	Medium	
Dicke von Stauss	Green leaves irregularly convoluted at margins.	8	Fan shaped	Medium	
Digitata Similar varieties: 'Palmata', 'Rottingdean'	Dark green, light-veined leaves, the 5 fingers of each widely splayed.	7	Fan shaped	Medium	Fast
Direktor Badke Similar variety: 'Christian'	Named after a former director of the Horticultural College at Wolbeck. Bushy ivy with red-purple stems densely set with soft green leaves with lighter veins. Each leaf has 3 circular lobes.	7	Heart shaped		Fast
Discolor	See 'Minor Marmorata'.				
Domino Similar varieties: 'Aalsmeer', 'Bodil', 'Fantasia', 'Pittsburgh Variegated'	Attractively spotted ivy, the pointed, 3-lobed leaves speckled and marbled cream and green. Hardy but needs shelter in exposed sites.	8	Ivy leaf	Medium	
Dragon Claw Synonym: 'Curley Q'	Robust, dramatic ivy, with lush, deeply curled leaves.	7	Fan shaped	Large	Fast
Dreizehn	See 'Professor Friedrich Tobler'.				
Duckfoot Synonym: 'Oakleaf'	Miniature ivy, with dense branching trails and 3-lobed green leaves like tiny ducks' feet.	7	Ivy leaf	Small	
Edison	The glossy green leaves are shield-shaped with 3 points, and slightly wavy.	8	Ivy leaf	Large	
Elegance	Bushy and branching ivy, with leathery leaves, 3 long lobes tapering to sharp points.	8	Ivy leaf	Medium	
Elfenbein	An unusual ivy. The rounded, slightly cupped leaves have a frilled or serrated variegated edge.	8	Fan shaped	Medium	Slow
Emerald Globe	Compact, bushy plant forming a globe of glossy green, deeply divided leaves with rounded tips.	8			Slow
Erecta	Upright shrubby ivy, resembling 'Congesta' but larger in all its parts.	7	Ivy leaf	Medium	Slow
Erin	Bushy, with deeply divided leaves.	8	Ivy leaf	Medium	
Ester	See 'Ingrid'.				
Eugen Hahn	Compact trails set with long leaves dappled and speckled with various shades of green, grey and cream.		Heart shaped	Medium	

Key:

Symbols in green indicate better than average performance

Ivy leaf | Heart shaped | Fan shaped | Diamond shaped | Curly/crested | Bird's-foot | Small | Medium | Large | Fast | Slow

Variegation	Winter Colour	Uses
Cream		
Cream-white		
Grey, cream		

Legend: Grafts · Climber · Trailer · Hanging baskets · Ground cover · Indoor pots · Outdoor pots · Topiary · Bonsai

'Domino'

'Duckfoot'

'Eugen Hahn'

Plant name	Description	Zone	Leaf shape	Leaf size	Rate of growth
Eva	Bushy variegated ivy, popular as house plant in Europe. Grey-green pointed leaves with bright cream margins.	8	Ivy leaf	Small	Fast
Excalibur Synonym: 'Bill Archer'	Named after the sword of King Arthur, from the narrow leaves, held in clusters with a fern-like effect.		Bird's-foot	Small	Fast
Fallen Angel	Compact ivy, with densely packed, spade-shaped leaves spiralling on stout trailing stems; new growths turn upwards.		Fan shaped	Small	
Fan Synonym: 'California Fan' Similar variety: 'Alpha'	Bushy, compact growth habit, trails well covered with soft apple-green leaves with prominent veins.	6	Fan shaped	Large	
Fantasia	Similar to 'Domino'.				
Feinfinger	Similar to 'Königer's'.				
Ferney	Graceful ivy of dense, branching growth.	8	Bird's-foot	Large	
Fiesta	Similar to 'Ivalace'.				
Filigran	Non-branching ivy with leaves so crimped and curled they look like frilly balls.	8	Curly/crested	Small	Slow
Flamenco	Similar to 'Ivalace'.				
Fleur de Lis	Outstanding green-leaved ivy, bushy with long trails. Prominent white leaf veins.	8	Bird's-foot	Large	Fast
Fluffy Ruffles	Outstanding and unusual house plant. Green leaves, with yellow veins, are deeply fluted like rosettes held on long pinkish stalks.	8	Curly/crested	Large	
Fringette	Green, 3-lobed leaves with long central lobe and crimped margins.	8	Fan shaped	Large	
Frosty	Miniature ivy, leaves mottled cream and green when young, later mottled shades of green. Bottle gardens.	8	Bird's-foot	Small	
Galaxy	Densely branching ivy forming a lacy mat over a small area or against a low wall. The green leaves are close to the stems.	7	Bird's-foot	Small	
Garland	Good pot plant with compact bushy growth, also suitable for ground cover in small areas. Rich green leaves, closely set, overlap along sturdy pink-green curving stems to give a garland effect.	7	Heart shaped	Large	
Gavotte	Similar to 'Brokamp'.				
Glache	Dense and bushy with variegated leaf margins. Similar to 'Adam' and 'Eva', but half their size.		Ivy leaf	Large	Fast

Key:

Symbols in green indicate better than average performance

Ivy leaf · Heart shaped · Fan shaped · Diamond shaped · Curly/crested · Bird's-foot · Small · Medium · Large · Fast · Slow

Variegation	Winter Colour	Uses						
Cream		⌇↕ (climber)	⌇↓ (trailer)	◒ (hanging baskets)	↤⌇↦ (ground cover)	⊔ (indoor pots)		⌇ (topiary)
		⌇↕	⌇↓	◒		⊔	⊔ (outdoor)	
		⌇↕		◒		⊔	⊔	
		+ (grafts)			↤⌇↦	⊔	⊔	
			⌇↓	◒	↤⌇↦	⊔	⊔	
			⌇↓			⊔	⊔	
		⌇↕	⌇↓		↤⌇↦	⊔	⊔	⌇
			⌇↓	◒		⊔	⊔	
		⌇↕	⌇↓	◒	↤⌇↦	⊔	⊔	
Cream		⌇↕	⌇↓	◒		⊔	⊔	⌇
		⌇↕	⌇↓	◒	↤⌇↦	⊔	⊔	⌇
			⌇↓	◒	↤⌇↦	⊔		⌇
Cream		⌇↕	⌇↓		↤⌇↦	⊔	⊔	

'Eva'

'Fluffy Ruffles'

Key:

+ Grafts   ⌇↕ Climber   ⌇↓ Trailer   ◒ Hanging baskets   ↤⌇↦ Ground cover   ⊔ Indoor pots   ⊔ Outdoor pots   ⌇ Topiary   ⊔ Bonsai

Plant name	Description	Zone	Leaf shape	Leaf size	Rate of growth
Glacier Similar variety: *H. helix hibernica* 'Maculata'	Popular and long-established ivy, one of the best among variegated kinds. The grey-green leaves have patches of silver-grey and white margins. Strong growth on red-purple stems.	7	Ivy leaf	Medium	Fast
Glymii Synonym: 'Tortuosa' Similar variety: 'Atropurpurea	Dense-growing ivy, excellent in arborescent form. In cold weather the glossy dark green leaves turn darker purple than any other ivy, with prominent light veins.	7	Ivy leaf	Medium	Fast
Gnome	See 'Spetchley'.				
Goldchild Similar variety: 'Choice'	Some clones are more robust than others. At its best, an outstanding golden ivy for home and garden use.	8	Ivy leaf	Medium	Slow
Gold Craft	Bushy ivy with plenty of trails set with lime-yellow leaves with irregular green splashes; older leaves turn all-green.	8	Ivy leaf	Medium	
Gold Dust	Outstanding and easy ivy, heavily variegated; similar to the better known 'Luzii'.	8	Ivy leaf	Medium	
Golden Ester	See 'Ceridwen'.				
Golden Ingot Synonym: 'Golden Inge'	Said to be the most beautiful of golden ivies. Best grown as indoor plant. Lemon-yellow and lime-green leaves.	8	Ivy leaf	Medium	
Golden Jubilee	See 'Goldheart'.				
Golden Kolibri	See 'Midas Touch'.				
Golden Snow	Short-jointed, branching ivy with 3-lobed leaves of green, grey-green, white and sometimes edged palest yellow.	8	Ivy leaf	Small	
Goldfinger	Similar to 'Goldstern'.				
Goldheart Synonyms: 'Golden Jubilee', 'Goldherz', 'Oro del Bogliasco'	Formerly incorrectly known as 'Jubilee'. 'Goldheart' is the best and brightest variegated climbing ivy. The dark green leaves on red-pink stems have large central splashes of clear yellow. Prune out branches that revert to green. Slow at first, then climbs quickly.	8	Ivy leaf	Medium	Fast
Goldherz	See 'Goldheart'.				
Goldstern Similar varieties: 'Goldfinger', 'Goldtobler', 'Sterntaler'	Misleading name as the thin leaves are lime-green rather than gold, with darker central splashes.	8	Bird's-foot	Medium	
Goldwolke	Strong-growing, with quilted and rounded leaves faintly variegated in the young stage.	8	Heart shaped	Large	Fast
Gracilis	Good for quick cover on walls or trees. The slender 5-pointed leaves, on wiry red-purple stems, turn wine-red in winter.	7	Ivy leaf	Small	Fast

Key:

Symbols in green indicate better than average performance

Ivy leaf	Heart shaped	Fan shaped	Diamond shaped	Curly/ crested	Bird's-foot	Small	Medium	Large	Fast	Slow

Variegation	Winter Colour	Uses								
White-grey		+	Climber	Trailer	Hanging baskets	Ground cover	Indoor pots	Outdoor pots	Topiary	
	✓		Climber			Ground cover				
Yellow			Climber	Trailer	Hanging baskets	Ground cover	Indoor pots	Outdoor pots	Topiary	
Yellow			Climber		Hanging baskets		Indoor pots	Outdoor pots		
Yellow		+	Climber	Trailer	Hanging baskets	Ground cover	Indoor pots	Outdoor pots	Topiary	
Yellow			Climber	Trailer	Hanging baskets		Indoor pots			
White-yellow							Indoor pots	Outdoor pots		
Yellow			Climber							
Lime-green							Indoor pots	Outdoor pots		
Yellow/lime-yellow			Climber	Trailer	Hanging baskets		Indoor pots	Outdoor pots		
	✓		Climber							

Key: + Grafts | Climber | Trailer | Hanging baskets | Ground cover | Indoor pots | Outdoor pots | Topiary | Bonsai

'Glymii'

'Goldchild'

Plant name	Description	Zone	Leaf shape	Leaf size	Rate of growth
Green Feather Synonym: 'Meagheri'	Outstanding ivy producing long thin trails that can be pinched out to induce branching. Narrow dark green, 3-lobed leaves.	8	🌿	⊙	
Greenfinger	Similar to 'Königer's'.				
Green Heart	Similar to 'Trustee'.				
Green Ripple Synonym: 'Hahn's Green Ripple'. Similar variety: 'Manda Fringette'	Outstanding and robust all-purpose ivy with bright deep green leaves, sharp and forward pointing with prominent pale green veins. Tinged copper in winter.	5	🍁	◼	🐇
Green Spear	See 'Triton'.				
Grey Arrow	See 'Pedata'.				
Hahn Self-Branching	See 'Pittsburgh'.				
Hahn's Green Ripple	See 'Green Ripple'.				
Hamilton	See *H. helix hibernica* 'Hamilton'.				
Harald	See 'Ingrid'.				
Harlequin	Bold leaf variegations of grey, yellow and cream.	8	🍃	◼	
Harrison	Tough and ultra-hardy. The dark green leaves netted with white veins become maroon in winter.	5	🍃	◼	
Harry Wood	See 'Modern Times'.				
Hastata	See 'Deltoidea'.				
Hazel	Variegated sport of 'Adam'. Named after Hazel Key, author of the Royal Horticultural Society's handbook on ivies.	8	🍃	⊙	
Heise Synonym: 'Dean'	All purpose, bushy ivy, with rounded leaves with colouring reminiscent of 'Glacier'. 3-lobed.	8		⊡	🐇
Helena	Unusual little ivy, with grey, green and white variegation on star-like leaves with long, curved central lobes.	7	🌿	⊙	
Helford River	Similar to 'Thorndale'.				
Helvetica	Bred in Switzerland. Triangular, shield-shaped leaves, rich dark green with white veins. Red winter colour.	7	🍃	⊡	
Heron	See 'Pedata'.				
Hibernica	See *H. helix hibernica*.				

Key:

Symbols in green indicate better than average performance

Ivy leaf	Heart shaped	Fan shaped	Diamond shaped	Curly/ crested	Bird's-foot	Small	Medium	Large	Fast	Slow

Variegation	Winter Colour	Uses								
	✓	+	⇕	⇕	◉		▽	▽	⇕	
	✓		⇕	⇕	◉	↔⋀↔	▽	▽		
Yellow-cream			⇕	⇕	◉		▽	▽		
	✓		⇕			↔⋀↔				
Cream-white							▽			
White-grey			⇕	⇕	◉	↔⋀↔	▽	▽	⇕	
White-grey			⇕		◉		▽	▽	⇕	
	✓		⇕	⇕		↔⋀↔	▽	▽		

+	⇕	⇕	◉	↔⋀↔	▽	▽	⇕	▽
Grafts	Climber	Trailer	Hanging baskets	Ground cover	Indoor pots	Outdoor pots	Topiary	Bonsai

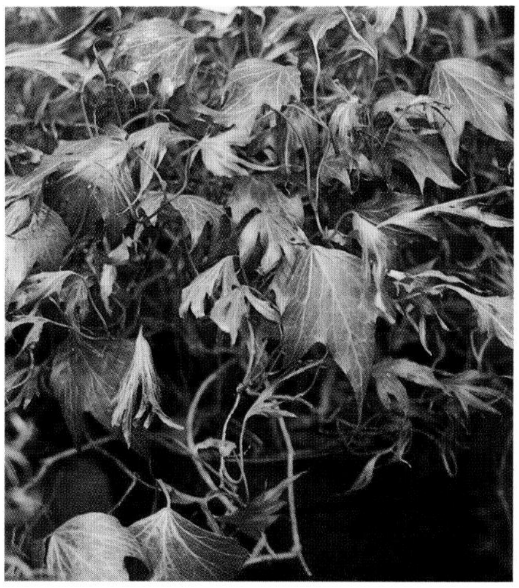

'Green Feather'

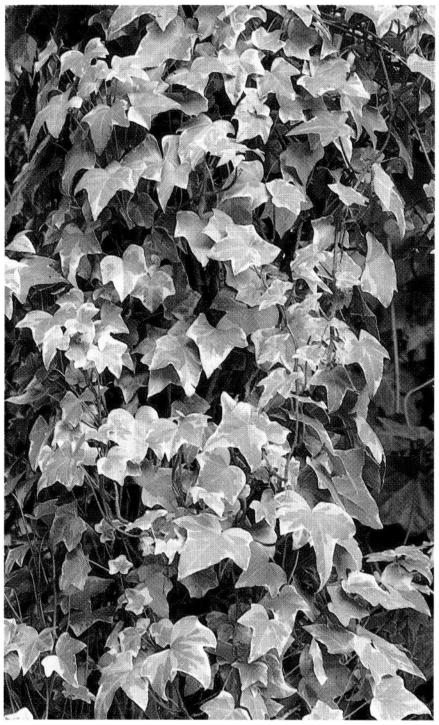

'Heise'

131

Plant name	Description	Zone	Leaf shape	Leaf size	Rate of growth
Holly	Similar to 'California'				
Imp	See 'Brokamp'.				
Ingobert	See 'Bruder Ingobert'.				
Ingrid Synonym: 'Ester' Similar varieties: 'Chicago Variegata', 'Harald'	Attractive, healthy ivy with grey-green leaves broadly variegated at the margins.	7	🍃 (Ivy leaf)	⊡ (Medium)	
Irish Gold	Bushy ivy, with slow-growing trails; overlapping pointed leaves, like shamrock.	8	🍃 (Ivy leaf)		🐢 (Slow)
Irish Lace	An outstanding example of the fine-fingered bird's-foot ivies developed from 'Königer's'. Very bushy and branching.	7	✴ (Bird's-foot)	⊡ (Medium)	🐢 (Slow)
Itsy Bitsy	Miniature ivy similar to 'Pin Oak'.				
Ivacurl	Similar to 'Ivalace'.				
Ivalace Synonyms: 'Lace Ivy', 'Lace Leaf', 'Lace Veil', 'Walaca' Similar varieties: 'Fiesta', 'Flamenco', 'Ivacurl', 'Parasol', 'Stuttgart', 'Tango'	Distinctive and popular ivy, of upward branching habit. Glossy, olive green leaves with ruffled margins that become copper in winter.	7	🍁 (Fan shaped)	⊙ (Small)	🐇 (Fast)
Jack Frost	Wavy-edged, 3-lobed leaves are brushed with silver.	7	🍃 (Ivy leaf)	⊞ (Large)	
Jersey Doris Similar variety: 'Sally'	Non-branching climber with speckled variegation on young leaves when grown in the open garden.	8	🍃 (Ivy leaf)		
Jubilee	Outstanding miniature ivy of densely branching habit. No relation to 'Goldheart'.	8	🫀 (Heart shaped)	⊙ (Small)	
Kleiner Diamant	See 'Little Diamond'.				
Knulch	See 'Big Deal'.				
Kobold Similar varieties: 'Spinosa', 'Waccamaw', 'Wichtel'	The name is German for goblin. Miniature self-branching ivy, overlapping leaves. Suitable for the rock garden.	7		⊙ (Small)	
Kolibri Similar varieties: 'Calico', 'Schafer Two' and 'Schafer Three'	Outstanding ivy, popular as a house plant and a good climber outdoors if sheltered. One of the whitest of variegated ivies, with green and grey flecks on creamy-white background.	8	🍃 (Ivy leaf)	⊙ (Small)	

Key:

Symbols in green indicate better than average performance

Ivy leaf	Heart shaped	Fan shaped
Diamond shaped	Curly/crested	Bird's-foot
Small	Medium	Large
Fast	Slow	

Variegation	Winter Colour	Uses
Cream		(Climber, Trailer, Hanging baskets, Ground cover, Indoor pots, Outdoor pots)
Yellow/ cream-yellow		(Climber, Indoor pots, Outdoor pots, Topiary)
		(Climber, Trailer, Hanging baskets, Ground cover, Indoor pots, Outdoor pots)
	✓	(Grafts, Climber, Trailer, Hanging baskets, Ground cover, Indoor pots, Outdoor pots, Topiary)
Silver		(Grafts, Trailer, Hanging baskets, Indoor pots, Outdoor pots)
Cream		(Climber)
Silver		(Trailer, Hanging baskets, Indoor pots, Outdoor pots, Topiary)
		(Ground cover, Indoor pots, Outdoor pots, Topiary)
White		(Grafts, Climber, Trailer, Hanging baskets, Indoor pots, Outdoor pots, Topiary)

'Irish Lace'

'Ivalace'

Legend:

+ Grafts   Climber   Trailer   Hanging baskets   Ground cover   Indoor pots   Outdoor pots   Topiary   Bonsai

133

Plant name	Description	Zone	Leaf shape	Leaf size	Rate of growth
Königer's Synonyms: 'Königer's Auslese', 'Mini Heron', 'Sagittifolia Minima' Similar varieties: 'Feinfinger', 'Greenfinger', 'Irish Lace', 'Miniature Needlepoint'	Excellent and useful ivy of dense branching growth and elegant, light green leaves divided into 5 slender lobes. See also 'Sagittifolia'.	7	Bird's-foot		Fast
Königer's Variegata	See 'Sagittifolia Variegata'.				
Kurios	Similar to 'Big Deal'.				
Lace Ivy, Leaf, Veil	See 'Ivalace'.				
Lady Kay Synonym: 'Lucy Kay'	Luxuriant bushy trailer densely set with dark green leaves.	7	Diamond shaped	Small	
Lalla Rookh Similar variety: 'New Ripples'	A strong, branching variety, with mid-green leaves, deeply cut and pointed with overlapping lobes prominently veined.	7	Fan shaped	Large	
Lancelot	Sport of 'Glacier', with strong climbing shoots. The grey and green leaves, irregularly variegated, have spear-shaped central lobes.	8	Bird's-foot	Medium	
La Plata	All-purpose miniature ivy with velvety, light green leaves with 3 rounded points.	8	Bird's-foot	Small	
Laubfrosch	Similar to 'Thorndale'.				
Lemon Swirl Synonym: 'Ustler Variegated'	Compact growth; slightly wavy, dark green leaves flecked with variegation between prominent dark green veins.	7	Ivy leaf	Medium	
Leo Swicegood	Bushy ivy with narrow, bright green leaves.		Diamond shaped	Small	
Light Finger	See 'Buttercup'.				
Lilliput	Miniature ivy of dense and bushy habit, with occasional long trails. The dark green, white-veined leaves are distinctively twisted.	8	Ivy leaf	Small	Slow
Little Diamond Synonym: 'Kleiner Diamant'	Outstanding small shrubby ivy, usually grown as pot plant but suitable for ground cover in rock gardens. Soft grey-green leaves, edged white, are closely set along short-branching stems.	8	Diamond shaped	Small	
Little Gem Similar variety: 'Arrowhead'	Branching ivy ideal for ground cover with spring bulbs; mid-green, 3-lobed leaves set close.	8	Ivy leaf	Small	
Little Picture	See 'Telecurl'.				
Longifolia	See 'Brokamp'.				

Key:

Symbols in green indicate better than average performance

Ivy leaf | Heart shaped | Fan shaped | Diamond shaped | Curly/crested | Bird's-foot | Small | Medium | Large | Fast | Slow

Variegation	Winter Colour	Uses							
		+	⌇	⌇	⬯	⟨⌇⟩	⬓	⬓	⌇
			⌇	⌇	⬯	⟨⌇⟩	⬓	⬓	
			⌇	⌇	⬯	⟨⌇⟩	⬓	⬓	
White			⌇	⌇	⬯	⟨⌇⟩	⬓	⬓	
			⌇	⌇	⬯	⟨⌇⟩	⬓	⬓	⌇
Cream					⬯		⬓	⬓	⌇
							⬓	⬓	⌇
					⬯		⬓	⬓	⌇
White	+					⟨⌇⟩	⬓	⬓	⌇
			⌇			⟨⌇⟩	⬓	⬓	

'Little Diamond'

'Leo Swicegood'

+	⌇	⌇	⬯	⟨⌇⟩	⬓	⬓	⌇	⬓
Grafts	Climber	Trailer	Hanging baskets	Ground cover	Indoor pots	Outdoor pots	Topiary	Bonsai

Plant name	Description	Zone	Leaf shape	Leaf size	Rate of growth
Lucy Kay	See 'Lady Kay'.				
Luzii, Lutzii, Luzzi, Lutzei	Outstanding and easy ivy, hardy in the open and surviving neglect as a house plant. Light grey-green marbled and speckled leaves.	7	🍃		
Macbeth	See 'Triton'.				
Maculata	See *H. helix hibernica* 'Maculata'.				
Manda Fringette	Similar to 'Green Ripple'.				
Manda's Crested Synonym: 'Curly Locks' Similar variety: 'Permanent Wave'	Introduced by W. A. Manda Inc. of New Jersey in 1940 as the first of curly-leaved ivies and still the best. The star-shaped, round-pointed leaves are soft pale green which in winter turn to shades of pink on the undersides, with coppery-red blotches on top.	7	🍁	◼	
Maple Leaf	Strong-growing ivy with mid-green leaves, divided and serrated like maple leaves.	7	🍃	◼	🐇
Maple Queen	Reliable and easily-grown ivy, dense-leaved and branching. Shiny, dark green leaves, with 3 blunt points, on red-purple stalks.	8/9	🍃	▪	
Margaret	See 'Pixie'.				
Marginata	See 'Cavendishii'.				
Marginata Elegantissima, Pulchella, Rubra	See 'Tricolor'.				
Marie Luise	Green-leaved ivy of bushy growth; the narrow lobes are so deeply divided that they appear like 3 separate leaflets.	8	⚜	·	
Marie Stauss	Long, pointed, grey-green leaves margined white.	8	🍁	◼	
Masquerade	Similar to 'Luzii'.				
Mathilde	Branching ivy with long trails well set with 5-pointed cream-edged leaves as broad as they are long.	8	🍃	◼	
Meagheri	See 'Green Feather'.				
Melanie	Discovered in 1980 as a shoot on 'Parsley Crested'. Bred by Beth Chatto. The frilled leaf margins have purple rims.	7	🍁	◼	
Merion Beauty Similar variety: 'Neilsonii'	Compact and reliable miniature ivy producing plenty of short, branching and well-clothed trails. Good foil for variegated ivies.	7	🍃	·	
Midas Touch Synonym: 'Golden Kolibri'	Attractive ivy, fully hardy but subject to weather damage and best as a house plant. Rich green leaves variegated.	8	🍂	◼	

Key:

Symbols in green indicate better than average performance

Ivy leaf	Heart shaped	Fan shaped	Diamond shaped	Curly/ crested	Bird's-foot	Small	Medium	Large	Fast	Slow

Variegation	Winter Colour	Uses						

Variegation	Winter Colour	Uses
Yellow		
Golden-yellow		
White		
Cream		

'Luzii'

'Meagheri'

Symbol	Grafts	Climber	Trailer	Hanging baskets	Ground cover	Indoor pots	Outdoor pots	Topiary	Bonsai

Plant name	Description	Zone	Leaf shape	Leaf size	Rate of growth
Midget Similar variety: 'Petit Point'	Handsome miniature ivy, forming a small cascade of trails densely set with bright green wavy leaves. Bottle gardens.	8	Bird's-foot	Small	Slow
Miniature Needlepoint Synonym: 'Needlepoint'	Elegant miniature ivy, bushy and with slender trails. The bright green leaves resemble those of 'Midget', but each of the 3 lobes is sharply pointed.	7	Bird's-foot	Small	
Mini Ester	Miniature ivy; leaves like 'Midget', but with variegated margins. Bottle gardens.	8	Bird's-foot	Small	
Minigreen	Similar to 'Trés Coupé'.				
Minima	See 'Spetchley'.				
Minor Marmorata Synonym: 'Discolor' Similar varieties: 'Dealbata', 'Peppermint', 'Tenerife'	Spotted ivy, white on dark green background, showing best on young leaves. Good in shade.	7	Ivy leaf	Medium	Fast
Miss Maroc Similar variety: 'Schimmer'	Climbing or trailing ivy of moderate vigour; star-shaped leaves with crimped margins.	7	Bird's-foot	Large	
Misty Synonyms: 'Silver Lace', 'Variegated Needlepoint'	Pointed, deeply lobed leaves with variegated margins and silver-grey veins radiating from the centre. Miniature.	8	Ivy leaf	Small	
Modern Times Similar varieties: 'Harry Wood', 'Woodii', 'Woodsii'	Semi-trailing ivy, suitable as climber on low walls and as a house plant. Soft, matt, apple-green leaves, covered with white veins, are suffused with copper in winter.	7	Heart shaped	Medium	
Mona Lisa	See 'Sagittifolia Variegata'.				
Mrs Pollock	A mid-green wall ivy whose pendent leaves have 5–7 forward-pointing lobes. In sun it sometimes shows gold colouring.	7	Fan shaped	Medium	Fast
Mrs Ulin Similar variety: 'Tomboy'	Small sturdy ivy with dark green leaves and white veins. Sometimes, as 'Tomboy', available in its arborescent form.	7	Heart shaped	Small	
Nebulosa	Discovered by Shirley Hibberd, the British ivy expert, in the village of Dwygyfylchi, North Wales. See also 'Thorndale'.	7	Ivy leaf	Small	
Needlepoint	See 'Miniature Needlepoint'.				
Neilsonii ('Neilson')	Similar to 'Merion Beauty', but larger leaves that take on copper-red tones in winter.	7	Ivy leaf	Medium	
Neptune	Fascinating ivy with strange leaves, reminiscent of underwater creatures, divided into tapering and twisting tentacles.	8		Medium	
New Ripples	Similar to 'Lalla Rookh'.				

Key:

Symbols in green indicate better than average performance

Ivy leaf · Heart shaped · Fan shaped · Diamond shaped · Curly/crested · Bird's-foot · Small · Medium · Large · Fast · Slow

Variegation	Winter Colour	Uses								
			Climber	Trailer			Indoor pots	Outdoor pots	Topiary	
							Indoor pots	Outdoor pots	Topiary	
		+				Ground cover	Indoor pots	Outdoor pots	Topiary	Bonsai
Cream			Trailer	Hanging baskets			Indoor pots	Outdoor pots	Topiary	
White				Trailer			Indoor pots	Outdoor pots		
White	+		Climber	Trailer	Hanging baskets			Indoor pots	Outdoor pots	
			Climber	Trailer	Hanging baskets		Indoor pots	Outdoor pots	Topiary	
	✓		Climber					Indoor pots		
			Climber	Trailer						
	✓		Climber	Trailer			Indoor pots	Outdoor pots		
			Climber	Trailer						
	✓		Climber	Trailer		Ground cover	Indoor pots	Outdoor pots	Topiary	
			Trailer	Hanging baskets			Indoor pots	Outdoor pots		

'Mrs Pollock'

'Neilson'

Legend:

+	Grafts
↕	Climber
↕	Trailer
⊕	Hanging baskets
↔	Ground cover
▽	Indoor pots
▽	Outdoor pots
↕	Topiary
⊔	Bonsai

Plant name	Description	Zone	Leaf shape	Leaf size	Rate of growth
Nice Guy	Asymmetrical leaves with variegated margins.	8	(bird's-foot)	(medium)	
Nigra	Similar to 'Atropurpurea' but with smaller leaves.				
Northington Gold	Triangular, 3-lobed leaves are green splashed with grey and clearly edged with variegated margins.	8	(ivy leaf)	(small)	
Oakleaf	See 'Duckfoot'.				
Olive Rose	Raised at Fibrex Nurseries in England. Hardy, dense and bushy ivy with dark green glossy leaves that curl under at the edges.	8	(fan shaped)	(small)	
Oro del Bogliasco	See 'Goldheart'.				
Ovata	See 'Deltoidea'.				
Palmata	Similar to 'Digitata' but the leaves are even more widely splayed and deeply divided and become brown-red in winter.	8	(fan shaped)	(medium)	(slow)
Paper Doll	Sport of 'Glacier', with similar colouring but with variable leaves; broad ivy or heart-shaped.	8		(small)	
Parasol	Similar to 'Ivalace'.				
Parsley Crested Synonyms: 'Crestata', 'Cristata', 'Parsley', 'Pice Lep', 'Rokoko' Similar varieties: 'Crispa', 'Old Lace'	Outstanding, strong-growing ivy with spectacular cascading trails. Shiny pale green leaves undulate on every plane and take on exceptional winter colours, clear pink-red on the undersides, the upper leaf sides suffused with dull crimson.	7	(fan shaped)	(large)	(fast)
Pedata Synonyms: 'Caenwoodiana', 'Grey Arrow', 'Heron'	Elegant and distinctive. Non-branching, climbing habit with leaves spaced well apart on the stems. Soft dark grey-green leaves with conspicuous white veins.	7	(bird's-foot)	(medium)	(fast)
Pennsylvanica	Climbing or trailing ivy with broad leaves having 5 shallow lobes.	7	(fan shaped)	(medium)	(fast)
Peppermint	Similar to 'Minor Marmorata'.				
Perkeo	Miniature ivy, with upright stems. Light green, puckered leaves, netted on red stems. Light crimson in winter colour.	7	(fan shaped)	(small)	(slow)
Perle	Oval leaves with clear variegation at the margins.	8	(diamond shaped)	(small)	
Permanent Wave	Similar to 'Manda's Crested'.				
Persian Carpet	Handsome, almost lobeless leaves have prominent white veins.	7	(heart shaped)	(large)	

Key:

Symbols in green indicate better than average performance

| Ivy leaf | Heart shaped | Fan shaped | Diamond shaped | Curly/ crested | Bird's-foot | Small | Medium | Large | Fast | Slow |

Variegation	Winter Colour	Uses								
		Climber	Trailer	Hanging baskets	Ground cover	Indoor pots	Outdoor pots	Topiary	Bonsai
Lime-yellow		⌇	⌇	⌂	⟲	⊔	⊔	⌇	
Yellow		⌇	⌇	⌂		⊔	⊔		
			⌇		⟲	⊔	⊔		
	✓	⌇	⌇						
Silver		⌇		⌂	⟲	⊔	⊔		
	✓	⌇	⌇	⌂	⟲	⊔	⊔	⌇	
	✓	⌇							
		⌇	⌇	⌂	⟲	⊔	⊔		
	✓	⌇	⌇			⊔	⊔		
Yellow		⌇	⌇			⊔	⊔	⌇	
		⌇	⌇		⟲				

Legend:

+	⌇	⌇	⌂	⟲	⊔	⊔	⌇	⊔
Grafts	Climber	Trailer	Hanging baskets	Ground cover	Indoor pots	Outdoor pots	Topiary	Bonsai

'Parsley Crested'

'Pedata'

Plant name	Description	Zone	Leaf shape	Leaf size	Rate of growth
Peter Similar variety: 'Serenade'	Branching bushy ivy, vaguely reminiscent of 'Goldheart' but with less well defined colouring of pale green and pale lemon or lime.	8	(ivy leaf)	(medium)	(slow)
Peter Pan	Unusual and delicate miniature with flexible, wiry stems.	8	(heart shaped)	(small)	
Petit Point	Similar to 'Midget'.				
Pialligo Jane	Short-jointed, compact ivy with 3-pointed, mid-green leaves speckled with creamy-white and an occasional all-white leaf.	8	(ivy leaf)	(small)	
Pice Lep	See 'Parsley Crested'.				
Pin Oak Similar varieties: 'Itsy Bitsy', 'Staghorn', 'Walthamensis'	Outstanding trailing ivy of dense growth, branching and with long trails. Pointed light green leaves cluster along red-purple stems. Window-boxes.	8	(bird's-foot)	(small)	(fast)
Pirouette	Unusual plant, unlike an ivy. The deeply waved leaves with raised veins curve around the stems.	8	(fan shaped)	(small)	
Pittsburgh Synonym: 'Hahn Self-Branching' Similar varieties: 'Chicago', 'Ray's Supreme'	Outstanding, all-purpose ivy, the ancestor of all branching ivies. Introduced in 1920 by Paul S. Randolph of Verona, Pennsylvania. It is short-jointed and branches from every node on the stems, forming a dense and bushy plant with green, 5-lobed and pointed leaves, sometimes copper-red in winter.	7	(ivy leaf)	(medium)	(fast)
Pittsburgh Variegated	Similar to 'Domino'.				
Pixie Synonym: 'Margaret'	Miniature ivy, branching and trailing and ideal for window-boxes and bottle gardens. The soft, light green leaves have lightly crimped edges. 'Pixie Dixie' trails even more.	7	(fan shaped)	(small)	
Plume d'Or	Tight, bushy miniature ivy bristling with thick, golden-green stems crowded with narrow green leaves. Bottle gardens.	7	(bird's-foot)	(small)	(fast)
Poetica	The poet's ivy, mentioned by Pliny. In the arborescent form it makes an unusual shrub, with bright green, shallow-lobed leaves. As a climber, it is stiff and upright.	7	(ivy leaf)	(large)	(fast)
Port Nancy	See 'Thorndale'.				
Preston Tiny	Similar to 'Très Coupé', but with sharply pointed lobes.				
Prima Donna	Compact branching ivy with bright green, white-splashed leaves.	8	(ivy leaf)	(small)	
Professor Friedrich Tobler Synonyms: 'Dreizehn', 'Weidenblattrig'	Bushy ivy with plenty of long trails. Mid-green leaves, the 3 narrow lobes often completely divided, are held close to the stems; tinged copper in winter.	7	(bird's-foot)	(small)	
Purpurea	See 'Atropurpurea'.				

Key:

Symbols in green indicate better than average performance

(ivy leaf)	(heart shaped)	(fan shaped)	(diamond shaped)	(curly/crested)	(bird's-foot)	(small)	(medium)	(large)	(fast)	(slow)
Ivy leaf	Heart shaped	Fan shaped	Diamond shaped	Curly/ crested	Bird's-foot	Small	Medium	Large	Fast	Slow

Variegation	Winter Colour	Uses							
Lime-yellow		+ Climber Trailer Hanging-basket					Indoor-pot	Outdoor-pot	Topiary
							Indoor-pot	Outdoor-pot	
Cream-white		Ground-cover Indoor-pot Outdoor-pot Topiary							
		+ Climber Trailer Hanging-basket Ground-cover (3ft/90cm apart)					Indoor-pot	Outdoor-pot	Topiary
		Trailer Hanging-basket					Indoor-pot	Outdoor-pot	Topiary
	✓	Climber Trailer Hanging-basket Ground-cover					Indoor-pot	Outdoor-pot	Topiary
		Climber Trailer Hanging-basket Ground-cover					Indoor-pot		Topiary
		Trailer Ground-cover					Indoor-pot	Outdoor-pot	Topiary Bonsai
		Climber Trailer					Indoor-pot	Outdoor-pot	
White		Indoor-pot Outdoor-pot							
	✓	Trailer Hanging-basket Ground-cover Indoor-pot Outdoor-pot							

Key:
+ Grafts | Climber | Trailer | Hanging baskets | Ground cover | Indoor pots | Outdoor pots | Topiary | Bonsai

'Plume d'Or'

'Poetica'

143

Plant name	Description	Zone	Leaf shape	Leaf size	Rate of growth
Quatermas	A freakish ivy with the undivided leaf margins tightly rolled inwards.	8	(fan)	Medium	
Ralf	Green-leaved ivy, in some winters turning bronze or yellowish with light crimson overlay.	7	(heart)	Medium	
Rauschgold	Star-shaped leaves slightly puckered with crimped margins and all-over variegation when young.	8	(fan)	Small	
Ray's Supreme	Similar to 'Pittsburgh'.				
Reef Shell	Oval, shell-like leaves with 3 vestigial, forward-pointing rounded lobes; cream stripes and margins.	8	(fan)	Medium	
Regency	Trailing ivy with faint yellow leaf-edges.	7	(ivy leaf)	Medium	
Rheingold	Outstanding climber, with clear yellow leaves, splashed in the centre with grey-green, sometimes yellow-grey-green marbling.	8	(ivy leaf)		
Ritterkreuz	Vigorous, fine-textured, trailing ivy. Dark green, long-pointed and maple-like leaves.	7	(bird's-foot)	Medium	Fast
Roehr Minor	See 'Walthamensis'.				
Rokoko	See 'Parsley Crested'.				
Romanze Synonym: 'Romance'	From Neuberg Monastery, excellent as a house plant. Velvety leaves, soft apple green, mottled yellow and dark green.	8	(fan)	Large	
Rona	See *H. helix hibernica* 'Rona'.				
Rottingdean	Similar to 'Digitata'.				
Rubaiyat	Robust ivy with attractive reddish winter colouring.	7	(ivy leaf)	Medium	Fast
Rumania	Similar to 'Baltica'.				
Rusche	Hardy trailing ivy, ideal for window-boxes and retaining walls. Bred at Neuberg Monastery. The dark green leaves, 3-lobed, pointed and deeply divided form ruched collars around the stems.	8	(ivy leaf)	Medium	Fast
Russelliana	Similar to 'Erecta'.				
Sagittifolia (Sagittaefolia)	The plant sold in UK is usually 'Königer's', and sometimes the 2 names are given as synonyms. The plants are *not* identical. US catalogues more correctly describe the arrowhead leaves of 'Sagittifolia' as shield-like, dark purple green, quite unlike 'Königer's'. Additionally, 'Sagittifolia' is non-branching and rather sparse.	7	(heart)	Medium	Fast

Key:

Symbols in green indicate better than average performance

| Ivy leaf | Heart shaped | Fan shaped | Diamond shaped | Curly/crested | Bird's-foot | Small | Medium | Large | Fast | Slow |

Variegation	Winter Colour	Uses
Yellow		
Cream		
Yellow		
Yellow		
		+
Lime-yellow		
	✓	

'Königer's' (see 'Sagittifolia')

'Ritterkruez'

+	Grafts
Climber	
Trailer	
Hanging baskets	
Ground cover	
Indoor pots	
Outdoor pots	
Topiary	
Bonsai	

145

Plant name	Description	Zone	Leaf shape	Leaf size	Rate of growth
Sagittifolia Variegata Synonym: 'Mona Lisa' Similar variety: 'Silver King'	One of the best variegated ivies, confusingly a form of 'Königer's' rather than 'Sagittifolia'. The arching trails are covered with elegant leaves of soft greyish-green, edged white, even in shade.	7	Bird's-foot	Small	
Salicifolia	See 'Brokamp'.				
Sally	Similar to 'Jersey Doris'.				
Sark	Similar to 'Deltoidea'.				
Schafer Two and **Three**	Similar to 'Kolibri'.				
Schimmer	Similar to 'Miss Maroc'.				
Scutifolia	Reliable and tough little ivy, clinging tightly to its support or running over the ground. Bright green and shiny leaves.	6	Heart shaped	Small	Fast
Serenade	Similar to 'Peter'.				
Shamrock	Sometimes known as the clover-leaf ivy from the dark green leaves that overlap among branching stems with short trails. Suffused with copper in cold weather. Bottle gardens.	7		Small	
Shannon	Pleated, deeply divided leaves are set on long trails.	7	Bird's-foot	Small	Fast
Silver King	Similar to 'Sagittifolia Variegata'.				
Silver Kolibri	See 'White Knight'.				
Silver Lace	See 'Misty'.				
Silver Queen	See 'Tricolor'.				
Sinclair Silver Leaf	Outstanding ivy for indoor use. Young leaves entirely cream and some remain so while others become mottled with light green and yet others turn all-green, giving a pale harlequin effect.	9	Ivy leaf	Small	
Small Deal	Strange little ivy with stiff upright stems. Contorted, puckered leaves with scalloped margins look like dark green flowers.	7	Fan shaped	Medium	
Spectabilis Aurea	Similar to 'Angularis Aurea'.				
Spectre	Branching and loosely sprawling ivy with mid-green, faintly variegated leaves that are deeply divided, pointed and twisting.	8	Fan shaped	Large	Slow
Spetchley Synonyms: 'Gnome', 'Minima'	The smallest of all ivies was discovered at Spetchley Park in Worcestershire, and has a doll's house charm. It will creep or climb in rock gardens, or paving cracks, amd make ground cover for bonsais and in dish, bottle or terrarium gardens.	7	Ivy leaf	Small	Slow
Spinosa	Similar to 'Kobold'.				

Key:

Symbols in green indicate better than average performance

| Ivy leaf | Heart shaped | Fan shaped | Diamond shaped | Curly/ crested | Bird's-foot | Small | Medium | Large | Fast | Slow |

Variagation	Winter Colour	Uses								
Cream-white		Climber	Trailer	Hanging baskets	Ground cover	Indoor pots	Outdoor pots	Topiary		
		Climber	Trailer		Ground cover					
	✓	+ Grafts	Trailer		Ground cover		Outdoor pots	Topiary	Bonsai	
			Trailer			Indoor pots	Outdoor pots	Topiary		
Cream		+ Grafts					Outdoor pots	Topiary		
			Trailer			Indoor pots	Outdoor pots		Bonsai	
White			Trailer	Hanging baskets		Indoor pots	Outdoor pots			
	✓	Climber			Ground cover	Indoor pots	Outdoor pots	Topiary	Bonsai	

Legend:

+	↕	↕	⬭	↔	⊔	⊔	ǀ	⊔
Grafts	Climber	Trailer	Hanging baskets	Ground cover	Indoor pots	Outdoor pots	Topiary	Bonsai

'Sagittifolia Variegata'

'Spetchley'

147

Plant name	Description	Zone	Leaf shape	Leaf size	Rate of growth
Star	Shapely branching ivy with 5-pointed, star-like leaves.	8	(Bird's-foot)	(Medium)	(Slow)
Sterntaler	Similar to 'Goldstern'.				
Stift Neuberg	Rare variety, difficult to propagate. The rounded, jade-green leaves on pink stems are variegated in the centre.	8	(Fan shaped)	(Medium)	(Slow)
Stuttgart	Similar to 'Ivalace', with larger and less curled leaves.				
Succinata	Rarely seen ivy, possibly the one described by Shirley Hibberd in 1872 as the 'amber leafed ivy'. Mainly dark dull-green, but on mature plants in full sun new growth is golden-amber.	7	(Ivy leaf)		(Fast)
Sulphurea	See *H. helix hibernica* 'Sulphurea'.				
Sweetheart	See 'Deltoidea'.				
Sylvanian	Similar to 'Brokamp'.				
238th Street	Yellow-veined green leaves. In arborescent form it still produces trailing adult growth.	5	(Heart shaped)	(Medium)	
Tango	Similar to 'Ivalace'.				
Tear Drop	Bushy ivy with pretty pear-shaped, smooth-margined leaves.	7	(Heart shaped)	(Medium)	
Telecurl Synonym: 'Little Picture'	A good, compact pot plant with trails of bright green, deeply convoluted leaves, in UK it needs shelter outdoors.	8	(Curly/crested)	(Small)	(Slow)
Tenerife	Similar to 'Minor Marmorata'.				
Tess	The UK variety appears similar to the original 'Tesselata' of the 1890s whose blunt-lobed leaves were netted with yellow veins. The US 'Tess' is described as having dark green, white-netted leaves.	7		(Medium)	(Fast)
Thorndale Similar varieties: 'Helford River', 'Laubfrosch', 'Nebulosa', 'Port Nancy', 'Welsomi', 'Wilson'	This and its similar varieties are fully hardy variations of the wild English ivy (*H. helix*). They show only minor differences in growth habit, leaf colour and shape.	7/6	(Ivy leaf)		
Tiger Eyes	Needs good light to show off the central yellow variegation.	8	(Bird's-foot)	(Medium)	
Tobler	See 'Professor Friedrich Tobler'.				
Tomboy	Similar to 'Mrs Ulin'.				
Tortuosa	See 'Glymii'.				

Key:

Symbols in green indicate better than average performance

Ivy leaf	Heart shaped	Fan shaped	Diamond shaped	Curly/crested	Bird's-foot	Small	Medium	Large	Fast	Slow

Variegation	Winter Colour	Uses					
		Climber	Hanging baskets		Indoor pots	Outdoor pots	Topiary
Cream			Hanging baskets		Indoor pots		
Gold	✓	Climber					
		Climber, Trailer	Hanging baskets	Ground cover	Indoor pots	Outdoor pots	
		Trailer			Indoor pots	Outdoor pots	
		Climber, Trailer	Hanging baskets		Indoor pots	Outdoor pots	
Yellow or white		Climber			Indoor pots	Outdoor pots	
		Climber, Trailer		Ground cover			
Yellow		Climber, Trailer	Hanging baskets		Indoor pots	Outdoor pots	

'Stift Neuberg'

'Succinata'

Legend:

+ Grafts   Climber   Trailer   Hanging baskets   Ground cover   Indoor pots   Outdoor pots   Topiary   Bonsai

149

Plant name	Description	Zone	Leaf shape	Leaf size	Rate of growth
Touch of Class	Outstanding new ivy, with dark green glossy leaves, finely crimped.	7	Ivy leaf	Small	
Transit Road	See 'Walthamensis'.				
Très Coupé Similar varieties: 'Minigreen', 'Preston Tiny'	A short-jointed ivy, eventually forming a dense, compact bush. Leaves variable, mostly deeply cut with long central lobe.	7			Slow
Tricolor	The only variegated ivy with dependable winter colour. The triangular leaves are cream-yellow, with central splashes of grey-green, and sometimes edged with pink which intensifies in cold weather. The sparse leaves show best against a wall.	7	Diamond shaped	Small	Slow
Trinity	Outstanding house plant. The 5-lobed leaves are cream-white with pale green veins, all pale green or mottled green and white.	9	Ivy leaf	Medium	
Tristram	An elegant branching ivy, with long trails. Slender, 3-pointed leaves, mid-green with grey-green patches and cream margins.	8	Ivy leaf	Small	
Triton Synonyms: 'Green Spear', 'Macbeth'	An untidy sprawling ivy, best in trailing positions. Each leaf is deeply divided and consists of 3–5 sharply pointed, twisting fingers with raised veins, pointing forwards; bright green on wine-red stalks. Sometimes incorrectly offered as 'Green Feather'.	7	Fan shaped	Large	
Troll	Miniature version of 'Triton'.	7	Fan shaped	Small	
Trustee Similar varieties: 'Cathedral Wall', 'Green Heart'	Vigorous ivy with triangular, rich glossy green leaves thickly clothing the stems.	7	Ivy leaf	Large	Fast
Tussie Mussie	Compact trailing ivy with rounded and divided leaves, whitish splashed with green.	8	Heart shaped	Small	
Ustler	Attractive bushy ivy densely covered with glossy dark green wavy leaves.	7	Ivy leaf	Large	
Ustler Variegated	See 'Lemon Swirl'.				
Variegated Needlepoint	See 'Misty'.				
Waccamaw	Similar to 'Kobold'.				
Walaca	See 'Ivalace'.				
Walthamensis Synonyms: 'Roehr Minor', 'Transit Road'	Miniature ivy, popular in US. Good climber and also forms dense ground cover about 4in. (10cm) high. The rounded, triangular leaves, soft dark green with white veins, are held on purple stems.	7	Ivy leaf	Small	Fast
Weidenblattrig	See 'Professor Friedrich Tobler'.				

Key:

Symbols in green indicate better than average performance

| Ivy leaf | Heart shaped | Fan shaped | Diamond shaped | Curly/ crested | Bird's-foot | Small | Medium | Large | Fast | Slow |

Variegation	Winter Colour	Uses						

'Très Coupé'

'Trinity'

	Grafts	Climber	Trailer	Hanging baskets	Ground cover	Indoor pots	Outdoor pots	Topiary	Bonsai
+									

Variation rows (left column labels):
- Cream/ yellow-pink
- Cream-white
- Cream
- White

Plant name	Description	Zone	Leaf shape	Leaf size	Rate of growth
White Knight Synonym: 'Silver Kolibri'	Remarkable and showy plant with broadly 3-pointed, slightly undulating leaves of a startling white, including the veins, with sharply defined, uneven dark green splashes at the margins and sometimes across the leaves. Liable to weather damage.	9	Fan	Large	
Wichtel	Similar to 'Kobold'.				
William Kennedy	Dense miniature ivy, with trailing stems. Blunt 3-lobed leaves edged white, green centres splashed with grey. Bottle gardens.	8	Ivy leaf	Small	
Williamsiana	Good pot plant. Grey-green leaves with undulating margins and 3 long points curling downwards. Margins strongly variegated.	8	Ivy leaf	Medium	
Wood(s)ii	See 'Modern Times'.				
Zebra	Outstanding for its striped leaves, splashed grey-green and cream-yellow with prominent, almost parallel veins.	8	Ivy leaf	Medium	
HEDERA HELIX HIBERNICA	The familiar Irish ivy has been popular for more than 100 years, as healthy dense ground cover in municipal landscapes throughout Europe and USA.	7	Ivy leaf	Large	Fast
Hamilton	Similar to *H. helix hibernica,* but with sculptural bronze-green leaves.	7	Ivy leaf	Large	Fast
Maculata	Similar to *H. helix* 'Glacier'.				
Sulphurea	Broad, slightly crumpled leaves are smaller than other *hibernica* forms, grey-green becoming grey as they mature, and with sulphur-yellow leaf margins.	7	Ivy leaf	Medium	Fast
Variegata	A form of *Hibernica* with some leaves unevenly splashed with primrose yellow and some all yellow. Many leaves remain all green.	7	Ivy leaf		Fast
HEDERA NEPALENSIS	The Himalayan ivy, found throughout South-East Asia, climbs to considerable heights. The toothed leaves, narrowly triangular, taper to long points and hang downwards from wine-red stems. They are dull green with grey markings along the veins.	7	Heart shaped	Medium	Fast
Suzanne	Collected in Nepal by Dr John Creech of the US National Arboretum. Slender elongated and dark green mottled leaves.	7	Bird's-foot	Medium	
HEDERA PASTUCHOVII	Ultra-hardy ivy first collected in Russia in the 1930s and again in the 1970s from the Caspian Forest area of Iran. The leathery and glossy, dark green leaves have smooth unbroken margins.	4	Heart shaped	Large	
HEDERA RHOMBEA	Fragile-looking but fully hardy ivy from Japan. The dark green leaves are carried on long wiry stalks.	7	Heart shaped	Medium	Fast
Pierot	Elegant and smaller variety of *H. rhombea,* with clinging growth habit. Named after Suzanne Pierot, the American ivy expert.	7	Heart shaped	Medium	

Key:

Symbols in green indicate better than average performance

Ivy leaf — Heart shaped — Fan shaped — Diamond shaped — Curly/crested — Bird's-foot — Small — Medium — Large — Fast — Slow

Variegation	Winter Colour	Uses						
White						Indoor pots		
White, grey		Trailer	Hanging baskets	Indoor pots	Outdoor pots			
White		Climber	Trailer	Hanging baskets		Outdoor pots		
Cream-yellow		Climber	Trailer	Hanging baskets		Outdoor pots	Topiary	
		Climber	Trailer	Ground cover	Indoor pots	Outdoor pots	Topiary	
		Climber	Trailer	Ground cover	Indoor pots	Outdoor pots		
Yellow		Climber		Ground cover	Indoor pots	Outdoor pots		
Yellow		Climber		Ground cover				
		Climber			Indoor pots	Outdoor pots		
	+	Climber			Indoor pots	Outdoor pots		
	✓	Climber			Indoor pots	Outdoor pots		
		Climber	Trailer		Indoor pots	Outdoor pots		
		Climber	Trailer		Indoor pots	Outdoor pots		

Legend: + Grafts · Climber · Trailer · Hanging baskets · Ground cover · Indoor pots · Outdoor pots · Topiary · Bonsai

Hedera helix hibernica

'Sulphurea'

153

APPENDIX

USEFUL ADDRESSES

The American Ivy Society, National Center for American Horticulture, Mount Vernon, VA 22121, USA. Secretary: Mrs Elizabeth Carrick, PO Box 520, West Carrollton, OH 45449

British Ivy Society, Hon. Secretary: Mrs Beryl Hutchin, 14 Holly Grove, Huyton, Merseyside L36 4JA. Tel: 051 489 1083

Hardy Plant Society, 10 St Barnabas Road, Emmer Green, Caversham, Reading RG4 8RA. Publishers of *The Plant Finder*

SUPPLIERS

US IVY SPECIALISTS

Angelwood Nursery, 12839 McKee School Road, Woodburn, OR 97071. Cat. free. Tel: 503 634 2233

Apple Tree Nursery, 133 Myrtle Bush Lane, Jems, FL 33960. Tel: 813 465 1747

Gilson Gardens, PO Box 277, Rt 20, Perry, OH 44081. Tel: 216 259 4845. Cat. free.

Homestead Division of Sunnybrook Farms, 9448 Mayfield Rd, Chesterland, OH 44026. Tel: 216 729 9838. Cat. $1.

Ivies of the World, PO Box 408, Weirsdale, FL 32195. Tel: 904 821 2201/2322. Cat. $1.50.

The Ivy Guild, Inc., 835 Simonds Road, PO Box 371, Williamstown, MA 01267. Tel: 413 458 5701

Logee's Greenhouses (MO), 55 North Street, Danielson, CT 06239. Tel: 203 774 8038

Meadowbrook Farm (MO), 1633 Washington Lane, Meadowbrook, PA 19046. Tel: 887 5900

Merry Gardens, PO Box 595, Camden, ME 04843. Cat. $1.

Schubert Nursery Inc., PO Box 858, Half Moon Bay, CA 94019

Stonesboro Nurseries, RD 2, Stoneboro, PA 16153. Tel: 814 786 7991

Ter-el Nursery, PO Box 112, Orefield, PA 18069. Tel: 435 5411

Vine Acres Nursery, Inc., PO Box 317, Clarcona, FL 32710. Tel: 407 886 5900

SUPPLIERS OF TOPIARY FRAMES, ETC

Chicago Botanic Garden, PO Box 400, Lake Cook Road, Glencoe, IL 60022. Tel: 312 835 5440

Cliff Finch's Zoo, 16923 N. Friant Rd, PO Box 54, Friant, CA 93626. Tel: 209 822 2315

Deborah A. Reich, 25 Schermerhorn Street, Brooklyn, NY 11201. Tel: 718 643 6146

Gardenworks, PO Box 112, Coloma, CA 95613. Tel: 916 622 3895

Irene's Topiary (MO), 3045 North Academy, Dept CIL, Sanger, CA 93657. Tel: 209 875 8447

The Kinsman Company (MO), River Road, Dept 451, Point Pleasant, PA 18950. Tel: 215 297 5613

Kenneth Lynch & Sons Inc. (MO), 78 Danbury Road, PO Box 488, Wilton, CT 06897. Tel: 203 762 8363

Kreations by Kristen, 6295 Curriers Road, Arcade, NY 14009. Tel: 716 492 2848

McGuire Topiary and Sculptural Designs, 1601 Gullford Avenue, Baltimore, MA 21201. Tel: 301 426 1267

Meadowbrook Farm (MO), 1633 Washington Lane, Meadowbrook, PA 19046. Tel: 887 5900

Natures Alley, 3020 Middefield Road, Redwood City, CA 94063. Tel: 415 367 9772

Noah's Ark (MO), PO Box 10213, Largo, FL 34643. Tel: 813 393 8830

Topiaries Unlimited, RD2, PO Box 40C, Pownal, Vermont 05261. Tel: 802 823 5536

Topiary Inc. (MO), 41 Bering Street, Tampa, FL 33606. Tel: 813 254 3229

Totally Topiary (MO), PO Box 191, Stockton, NJ 08559. Tel: 609 397 2314

Vine Arts (MO), PO Box 03014, Portland, OR 97203. Tel: 503 289 7505

UK IVY SPECIALISTS

Fibrex Nurseries Ltd., Honeybourne Road, Pebworth, Nr Stratford-upon-Avon, CV37 8XT. Tel: 0789 720788

Whitehouse Ivies, Tolleshunt Knights, Maldon, Essex CM9 8EZ. Tel: 0206 24077. Nursery and small ivy garden.

UK NURSERIES

Barncroft Nurseries, Dunwood Lane, Longsdon, Stoke-on-Trent, Staffs ST9 9QW. Tel: 0538 384310/372111

Burncoose and South Downs Nursery, Gwennap, Redruth, Cornwall TR16 6BJ. Tel: 0209 861112

Hillier Nurseries Ltd., Ampfield House, Nr Romsey, Hampshire SO51 9PA. Tel: 0794 68733

Langthorn's Plantery, Little Canfield, Dunmow, Essex CM6 1TD. Tel: 0371 2611

Mallorn Gardens, Lanner Hill, Redruth, Cornwall TR16 6DA. Tel: 0209 215931

The Margery Fish Nursery, East Lambrook Manor, East Lambrook, S. Petherton, Somerset. Tel: 0460 40328

Perryhill Nurseries, Hartfield, Sussex TN7 4JP. Tel: 0892 77377

Roskellan Nursery, Maenlay, Helston, Cornwall, TR12 7QR. Tel: 0326 572657

Scotts Nurseries (Merriott) Ltd., Merriott, Somerset TA16 5PL. Tel: 0460 72306

Unusual Plants, Beth Chatto Gardens, Elmstead Market, Colchester, Essex CO7 7DB. Tel: 0206 222007

WORLDWIDE IVY SUPPLIERS

Australia:
Andreasen's Wholesale Nursery, Hollywood Drive, Lansvale, New South Wales 2166

Glenvale Plant Propagators, 586 Yatala Vale Road, Yatala Vale, South Australia 5126

Belgium:
Prost P.V.B.A., Antwerpsesteenweg 54, 2340 Beerse

Jan Sproyt, Mostrnveld 50, 9360 Buggenhout. Tel: 052/33 37 76

Van Pelt Nurseries, Liersebaan 194, 2580 Putte Mechelen

France:
Patrick Nicolas Nursery, 8 Sentier du Close Madame, 92190 Meudon. Tel: 16 (1) 45 34 09 27

Les Jardins de Valloires, 80120 Argoules. Tel: 22 23 53 55

Germany:
Neuberg Monastery Nursery, Heidelberg

Ireland:
Regional Nurseries, Sandyford Road,
Dundrum, Dublin 16

Italy:
Grandi Vivai Pozzi, Via XX Settembre 4, 13051
Biella

Fratelli Margheriti, Monte San Paolo 40, 53043
Chiusi, Siena

Piante Mati, Via Bonellina 49, 51020 Pistoia

Tor San Lorenzo, Via Campo di Carne 51,
00040 Tor San Lorenzo Areda, Roma

Japan:
Green Supply Saito, 42-4425-1 Ueno, Inakita,
Saito City, Miyazaki Prefecture. Tel: 0983 43
5619

Ivy Japan, 1-35 Hirano, Nagasaki City,
Nagasaki Prefecture

Ivy Toyo (Toyo Engei Co.), 3-3-39 Gakwen-
higashi, Kodaira City, Tokyo.Tel: 0423 45 3030

Koganei-en, 4-10-15 Nukuimininami-machi,
Koganei-shi, Tokyo 104

Shibamichi, 948 Akayama, Kawaguchi-shi,
Saitama 333

Toyo Zoen Doboku Co. Ltd., Nichirei
Akashicho Building, 6-4 Akashi-cho, Chuo-
ku, Tokyo 104

The Netherlands:
Pieter Zwynenburg JR, Halve Raak 18, 2771
AD Boskoop. Tel: 01727-18474

New Zealand:
Blue Mountain Nurseries, 99 Bushy Hill Street,
Tapanui, West Otago. Tel: 03 20 48250.
Comprehensive collection.

Norway:
Odegards Plantesalg, Isvik, N-5574 Skjold.
Small selection of the hardiest.

South Africa:
Contact the South African Institute of
Nurserymen, 214 Volkskas Building, Market
Street, Johannesburg 2001

PLACES TO SEE IVY

United States:
American Horticultural Society, River Farm
Headquarters, PO Box 0105, Mount Vernon,
VA 22121. Tel: 703 768 5700. Hardiness tests.

Angelwood Nursery, 12839 McKee School
Road, Woodburn, OR 97071. Tel: 503 634
2233. American Ivy Society Regional Standard
Reference Collection.

Arnold Arboretum, The Arborway, Jamaica
Plain, MA 02130. Tel: 617 524 1718

Brooklyn Botanic Garden, 1000 Washington
Avenue, Brooklyn, NY 11225. Tel: 718 622
4433

Chicago Botanic Gardens, Chicago, IL.
Tel: 312 835 5440. Hardiness tests.

Duke Gardens Foundation, Inc., PO Box
2030, Highway 206 South, Somerville,
NJ 08676. Tel: 201 722 3700. Good examples
of ivy trained formally.

Geoge Landis Arboretum, Esperance, NY.
Tel: 518 875 6936. Hardiness tests.

Longwood Gardens, PO Box 501,
Route 1, Kennett Square, PA 19348.
Tel: 215 388 6741. Outstanding topiary.

Meadowbrook Gardens, Virginia

Mendocino Coast Botanical Gardens, 18820
Highway One, PO Box 1143, Fort Bragg,
CA 95437. Tel: 707 964 4352. American Ivy
Society Regional Standard Reference
Collection.

San Diego Zoo, Balboa Park, San Diego. Life-
size topiary animals.

United Kingdom:
Chatsworth House, Bakewell, Derbyshire
DE4 1PT. Tel: 0246 582204. Ivy topiary.

Coutts & Co., 440 Strand, London WC2.

Erdigg Hall (National Trust. Head gardener:
Glyn Smith), Nr Wrexham, Clwyd, LL13 0YT,
N. Wales. Tel: 0978 355314. National
Collection of ivies, 100 varieties on brick wall
870ft (265m) long. Established from cuttings
from Wisley.

GLC Parks Department Nursery, Avery Hill
Park, Bexley Road, London SE9. Collection of
200 ivy varieties.

Glasgow Botanic Gardens, 730 Great Western
Road, Glasgow, Strathclyde, Scotland. Tel:
041 334 2422

Harlow Car Gardens, The Northern
Horticultural Society, Crag Lane, Harrogate,
N. Yorkshire. Tel: 0423 65418

Highgate Cemetery, Chester Road, London
N19, and Nunhead Cemetery, Linden Grove,
London SE15. Mostly common ivy –
romantic, evocative.

Liverpool University Botanic Gardens, Ness,
South Wirral, Cheshire L64 4AY. Tel: 051 336
2135/7769

Northumberland County Council, Kirkley
Hall, Ponteland, Newcastle-upon-Tyne,
Northumberland. National Collection of ivies
(Mr R. McParlin).

Polesden Lacey (National Trust), Nr Dorking,
Surrey RH5 6BD. Tel: 0372 58203. Ivy wall.

Powys Castle, Welshpool, Powys, Wales SY21
8RF. Tel: 0938 554336. Golden ivy hedge and
ivies in conservatory.

Royal Botanic Gardens, Kew, Richmond,
Surrey TW9 3AB. Tel: 081 940 1171.
Collection on wall behind the Order beds and
ivy hedge around the Palm House.

The Royal Horticultural Society's Gardens,
Wisley, Woking, Surrey GU23 6QB. Tel: 0483
224234

Temple Newsam, Leeds City Council, Leeds,
W. Yorkshire. Tel: 0532 645535

Canada:
University of British Columbia Botanical
Garden, 6804 Southwest Marine Drive,
Vancouver, BC U6T 1W5

Germany:
Neuberg Monastery, Heidelberg, Germany

Ireland:
National Botanic Garden, Glasnedin,
Dublin 9

Japan:
Garden Wako, 3-2-20 Yamamotonaka,
Takarazuka-shi, Hyogo 665

Switzerland:
The Botanical Gardens, Basle. Ivy garden.

BIBLIOGRAPHY

Bean, W. J. *Trees and Shrubs Hardy in the British Isles* (1973 ed)

Burbidge, F. W. *Domestic Floriculture* (1875)

Cassell's Popular Gardening (1870s)

Fish, Margery *Ground Cover Plants* (1964)

Floral World and Garden Guide Ed. Shirley Hibberd (1864, 1866, 1867, 1875)

Gallup, Barbara and Reich, Deborah *The Complete Book of Topiary* (1987)

Gardener's Chronicle (30 September 1867)

Grüber, Garry *Characteristics, Culture and Uses of Winter-hardy Hedera Species and Cultivars* (1983)

Hassard, Annie *Floral Decorations for the Dwelling House* (1875)

Hibberd, Shirley *The Ivy – Its History, Uses and Characteristics* (1872)

Ivy: (Journal of the British Ivy Society)

The Ivy Journal (American Ivy Society)

Key, Hazel *Ivies* (Royal Horticultural Society, Wisley Handbook 1978)

Lloyd, Christopher *Foliage Plants and Ground Cover Plants* (1973)

Marsh, T. C. *Flower and Fruit Decoration* (1862)

Page, Russell *The Education of a Gardener* (1962)

Pierot, Suzanne Warner *The Ivy Book* (1974)

Reich, Deborah 'Ivy: A Symbol of Mirth Emerges from Shadow' *American Horticulturist,* December 1989

Robinson, William *The Wild Garden* (1870)

Rose, Peter Q. *Ivies* (Blandford, revised edn. 1990); 'The Poet's Ivy' in *The Garden,* February 1985

Segall, Barbara, 'The Ivy and the Holly' in *Hortus,* no. 12, Winter 1989

Sulgrove, Sabina Mueller, 'Versatile New Ivies' *Garden Design* Autumn 1967; *A Selection of Ivies for Landscape Use,* The American Ivy Society, 1987

Thomas, Graham Stuart *Plants for Ground Cover* (1970)

AUTHOR'S ACKNOWLEDGEMENTS

The aim of this book is to encourage in professional and amateur landscapers and gardeners a more adventurous and imaginative approach to the great variety of available ivies. For technical and botanical information and for descriptions of ivies of which I have no first-hand experience, I am indebted to Peter Q. Rose's book *Ivies,* to Hazel Key's Wisley Handbook, *Ivies,* and to the catalogues of Ivies of the World and Merry Gardens in the USA, and Fibrex Nurseries and Whitehouse Ivies in the UK. I have also made much use of the publications of the British Ivy Society and the American Ivy Society.

I wish also to thank the following people for their help: M. Ciais, T. I. Croosen, S. Gavini, Denis and Margaret Hughes, Dr L. Haegi, S. K. Hall, Bernard S. Jackson, Hazel Key, Anne Lederer, Knut Lono, P. F. Lumley, Maria Viola Maori, Tony May, Dr E. Charles Nelson, Anne Philley, Michael Reece, R. Saquet, David Tarrant, Alan Thompson, Ronald Whitehouse, Peter Wirtz. Special thanks to Peggy Sadler, Philippa Lewis, Lizzie Boyd and Rowena Skelton-Wallace for all their help.

PICTURE ACKNOWLEDGEMENTS

Arcaid 26 (Viv Porter), 27, 36 (Lucinda Lambton), 57 (John Croce); Ardea 9; A-Z Botanical Collection 139 *bottom,* 143 *bottom,* 153 *top*; Peter Baistow 2 *right,* 100, 110, 141 *bottom*; Bodleian Library, Oxford 13; Bridgeman Art Library 12, 19, 94; Christie's Colour Library 95; Edifice 8, 38, 39, 59, 60, 61, 65, 74, 78; Elizabeth Whiting & Associates 86, 91, 92, 93; Fibrex Nurseries 145 *bottom* (Angela Tandy); Fine Art Photographs 2 *above*; Garden Picture Library i (Perdereau/ Thomas), ii (Roger Hyam), vi (Henry Dijkman), 3 (Jerry Pavia), 4 (Juliet Wade), 11 *right* (Brian Carter), 16 (Roger Hyam), 21 (Nigel Temple), 22 (John Neubauer), 28 (Clive Boursnell), 30 (Caroline Arbour), 31 *left* (Ann Kelly), 32 (Steven Wooster), 40 (Jerry Pavia), 45 (Joanne Pavia), 49 (Ron Suther- land), 62 (Derek Fell), 66, 71 *right* (Joanne Pavia), 72 (Ron Sutherland), 75 (John Glover), 77 (Neil Holmes), 79 (Marijke Heuff), 80 (John McCarthy), 83 (John Miller), 85 (Brigitte Thomas), 90 (John Miller), 96 (Geoff Dann), 98 (John Miller), 99 (Elizabeth Strauss),102 (Marijke Heuff), 103 (Joanne Pavia), 104 (Brigitte Thomas), 107, 109 (Perdereau/ Thomas), 115 *bottom* (J.S. Sira), 133 *top,* 149 *bottom,* 153 *bottom* (John Glover); John Glover 117 *bottom,* 119 *top,* 127 *bottom,* 133 *top,* 139 *top*; Martin & Dorothy Grace 7, 10, 25; Andrew Lawson 23, 84, 129 *bottom,* 137 *top,* 147 *top,* 149 *top*; Mansell Collection 15, 18 *right,* 88, 89; S. & O. Mathews 24, 33; Tania Midgley v (design by Helen Dillon), 76, 115 *top*; National Trust 46; Natural Image 10 *right,* 121 *middle,* 135 *top*; Hugh Palmer viii, 31 *top,* 41, 42, 48, 50 *right*; Photos Horti- cultural 37, 52, 121 *top, bottom,* 123 *top,* 127 *top,* 133 *bottom,* 137 *bottom,* 145 *top*; San Diego Zoological Garden 64, 67, 71 *left;* Donald Smith 6, 44; Harry Smith 34, 35, 47, 56, 58, 101, 105, 107, 117 *top,* 119 *bottom,* 123 *bottom,* 125, 129 *top,* 131, 135 *bottom,* 141 *top,* 143 *top,* 147 *bottom,* 151; Sotheby & Co. 14; Amoret Tanner Collection 20.

Line illustrations Tig Sutton
Zone maps, chart design assistance and endpapers David Bootle